In the fall of 1948 H. L. Mencken top of his unmatchable form (he had spoken at a meeting of the American Philosophical Society in Philadelphia only a little while before), suffered a stroke. He soon recovered his physical vigor, but writing was for him a thing of the past. Some months before his death, in going through some papers that he was putting in order for deposit in his beloved Enoch Pratt Free Library in Baltimore, his long-time secretary discovered these Note-books. Mencken meant to publish them, as he makes clear in the preface, which also describes them better than I can.

Suffice it to say that here is one more gen-erous sampling of the old Mencken battling fearlessly for the freedom and dignity of the individual and for the general decencies of life and attacking all that seems fundamentally

Read the preface and note that this book is precisely what its title suggests; it consists of hundreds of notes—some only a few lines in length, some running to several pages, all reflecting a rigorous and exhilarating mind and personality. It may be a long time before another like him crosses our path.

BOOKS BY
H. L. Mencken

THE AMERICAN LANGUAGE

THE AMERICAN LANGUAGE: *Supplement One*

THE AMERICAN LANGUAGE: *Supplement Two*

HAPPY DAYS ⎫ *which, taken together,*

NEWSPAPER DAYS ⎬ *constitute* THE DAYS

HEATHEN DAYS ⎭ OF H. L. MENCKEN

A NEW DICTIONARY OF QUOTATIONS

TREATISE ON THE GODS

CHRISTMAS STORY

A MENCKEN CHRESTOMATHY

(with selections from the *Prejudices* series, *A Book of Burlesques, In Defense of Women, Notes on Democracy, Making a President, A Book of Calumny, Treatise on Right and Wrong,* with pieces from the *American Mercury, Smart Set,* and *Baltimore Evening Sun,* and some previously unpublished notes)

MINORITY REPORT: *H. L. Mencken's Notebooks*

These are Borzoi Books

PUBLISHED BY *Alfred A. Knopf* IN NEW YORK

MINORITY REPORT

H. L. Mencken's Notebooks

MINORITY
REPORT

H. L. Mencken's

Notebooks

1956

ALFRED · A · KNOPF

NEW YORK

L. C. catalog card number: 56–7717

© *Alfred A. Knopf, Inc., 1956*

THIS IS A BORZOI BOOK,
PUBLISHED BY ALFRED A. KNOPF, INC.

FIRST EDITION

PREFACE

THIS is not a book, but a notebook. It is made up of selections chosen more or less at random from the memoranda of long years devoted to the pursuit, anatomizing and embalming of ideas. Ever since my earliest attempts as an author I have followed the somewhat banal practise of setting down notions as they come to me, sometimes in the form of hasty scrawls, unintelligible to anyone else, and then throwing these notes into a bin. Out of that bin have come a couple of dozen books and pamphlets and an almost innumerable swarm of magazine and newspaper articles, but still the raw materials kept mounting faster than I could work them up, so I am printing herewith some select samples of them, partly for the purpose of getting them off my hands and my conscience, and partly in the hope that some of them, at least, may enkindle an occasional reader to more orderly and profitable lucubrations.

As I grow older I am unpleasantly impressed by the fact that giving each human being but one life is a bad scheme. He should have two at the lowest—one for observing and studying the world, and the other for formulating and setting down his conclusions about it. Forced, as he is by the present irrational arrangement, to undertake the second function before he has made any substantial progress with the first, he limps along like an athlete only half trained. His competitors, to be sure, are in the same case, and in consequence his inadequacy tends to be concealed, but it is there none the less, and I sometimes suspect that it may be the main cause of the blowsy vacuity which marks so much of the so-called thinking of mankind. What ails that thinking, two times out of three, is simply its disregard of large categories of essential fact—obvious, but not yet observed. Half in the light and half in the dark, the sage takes refuge in his feelings, which is almost as if a surgeon employed to cut off a leg should do so.

I here open the way, of course, for an inevitable riposte, and since I know no way to dispose of it I am forced to admit its appositeness. But it is at all events something (or so I believe) to recognize an infirmity when it exists, and not try to exorcise it by calling it health. The most we can hope for in this world is to do the best we can with the miserable means at hand, and that is all I pretend to do by these presents. They are offered as notes merely, and not as anything else. If I could begin another life at my Septuagesima I might have some expectation of developing them (and the thousands of like ones that still lie in my bin) into something properly describable as a coherent and even elegant system, but as it is I'll have to spend my time post-mortem either bawling liturgical music (which I greatly dislike) or boiling in oil (which no one speaks well of). Thus I make no apology for printing my brief and often crude memoranda. Much better men have done the same to public edification and applause, for example, Blaise Pascal, François de la Rochefoucauld and F. W. Nietzsche, and also some who were perhaps definitely worse, for example, Bronson Alcott and Henry Ward Beecher. The form is not common in this incomparable republic, but there are a number of other serviceable things that are not common here, and a few of them are hinted at in the pages following.

H. L. Mencken

Baltimore

MINORITY REPORT

H. L. Mencken's Notebooks

H·L·M

1

We must respect the other fellow's religion, but only in the sense and to the extent that we respect his theory that his wife is beautiful and his children smart.

2

A dull, dark, depressing day in Winter: the whole world looks like a Methodist church at Wednesday night prayer-meeting.

3

In a country of pushers and yearners, what a joy it is to meet a man who envies no one and wants to be nothing that he is not!

4

The really astounding thing about marriage is not that it so often goes to smash, but that it so often endures. All the chances run against it, and yet people manage to survive it, and even to like it. The capacity of the human mind for illusion is one of the causes here. Under duress it can very easily convert black into white. It can even convert children into blessings.

5

WOMEN yield to the current fashions, however preposterous, because they are too realistic to try to conceal their natural human inclination to dress up, to strike the public eye with arresting gauds, to give a show of wealth and consequence, always impressive to people in general. Women know how much such a display is admired and envied, and how much envy may be worth—in deference and respect.

6

THE EFFORT to get rid of cruelty in punishment has made imprisonment the principal and indeed almost its only legal form. But imprisonment itself is far more cruel than most persons suspect. I well recall visiting the Maryland Penitentiary during the depths of the Depression and seeing hundreds of men sitting about the idle shops, with all day on their hands and nothing whatever to do. Some of them tried to occupy themselves by making various trivial gimcracks, but the majority simply sat with folded hands, staring into space. It was a dreadful picture of man's unwitting inhumanity to man. Brady, the warden, told me that all of the more unstable men, a large element in any prison, were on the verge of insanity, and that many of them crossed the line. He was rapidly finding himself in charge of a lunatic asylum rather than a penitentiary. In the days of Warden John F. Weyler the inmates of the Maryland Penitentiary all worked in the shops, and most of them earned much cash for exceeding their moderate daily stints. But the labor unions procured the adoption of national legislation that put prison-made goods under the ban, and the Depression did the rest. It was not until war industries were set up in all American prisons, in 1940 or thereabout, that the men were released from their demoralizing idleness.

Our rules of evidence, like our system of punishments, are full of irrationalities. They exclude a great many pertinent facts, for example, what sort of man is accused of the crime, and what sort suffered from it. The jury is supposed to hear and know nothing about the record of the accused, which is not mentioned until he has been found guilty and the judge is ready to sentence him. In Maryland, where persons charged with crime, including even capital crime, may elect to be tried by a judge or judges without a jury, this leads to frequent absurdities. The judge usually knows quite well what the accused's record is, but he is supposed to be ignorant of it until he has announced his verdict.

I long ago suggested that, in trials for murder or assault, it should be competent for the defense to introduce testimony showing the character of the victim. Certainly it is absurd to inflict the same punishment for killing or mauling a perfectly decent and innocent person, and doing the same to a gunman or other professional ruffian. I am willing to go further. That is, I am willing to admit evidence to show that the victim, though perhaps not a criminal himself, was of such small social value that his death or injury was no appreciable public loss. But in this field the lawyers and judges cling to the idea of equality before the law, though it has been cheerfully abandoned elsewhere, for example, in the field of labor relations. In the South, where most murder victims are Negroes, a very plain, though not official distinction is made between killing a white man and killing a Negro. It is dealt with at length in Gunnar Myrdal's "American Dilemma."

The recurrent effort to eliminate criminal stocks by sterilizing criminals is opposed violently by sentimentalists, and also by the pseudo-scientists who argue factuously that character is not inheritable. Common experience shows that it is, and all really scientific evidence supports the experience. The late Judge Frederick Bausman of Seattle (1861–1931) proposed after World War I that a sharp distinction be made between murderers whose crimes are of such a character that any normal persons, under the circumstances, might be imagined committing them, and murderers who kill strangers for gain. The former he proposed to treat tenderly, but for the latter he advocated certain death. This Bausman was an intelligent man—his book, "Let France Explain," published in 1922, was one of the first effective challenges to the official theory as to the origins of World War I—but his proposals got very little notice.

The objection to sterilizing criminals is mainly theological, and hence irrational. On a more respectable level it is sometimes argued that a criminal may not transmit his evil traits to offspring, and in support thereof it is pointed out that he sometimes has quite respectable sibs. But this is begging the question, for no one proposes to sterilize his brothers and sisters, but only the man himself. Certainly the chances that he will produce criminal children are sufficiently strong to justify subjecting him to the trivial injury and inconvenience of sterilization. On the one hand the sentimentalists argue that crime is a disease, and on the other hand they deny that it runs in families. All human experience is against this. Nine out of ten professional criminals come from families that are plainly abnormal. Even if it be argued that their criminality is thus the product of environment rather than of heredity, it follows that the environment they themselves provide for children is very likely to produce more criminals.

The theory that crime is caused by poverty is not supported by the known facts. The very poor, in fact, tend to be just as law-abiding as the rich, and perhaps more so. To argue otherwise is to libel multitudes of people who keep to decency under severe difficulties, and in the face of constant temptation.

7

ONE OF the chief objects of medicine is to save us from the natural consequences of our vices and follies. The moment it becomes moral it becomes quackery. A scientific physician should have no opinion about the ethical standards and deserts of his patient.

8

A STRONG government always wars on the superior man. Its regimenting of the inferior goes on too, but is harmless; they can't be made worse. But its enmity to the superior does real damage. Converting a million serfs into slaves merely changes their name, but wrecking one potential Goethe or Darwin may be a capital disaster to the race.

9

THE PREJUDICE against adultery arises from the inferior man's fear that he can't hold his woman. This fear, in the presence of competition from a better man, is certainly not without reason. On the upper levels adultery is measurably less disreputable, and in circles where egoism is notably powerful, as among artists, it tends to vanish. It would be interesting to speculate about the debt civilization owes to the complaisance of married women. That complaisance has not only produced a great many able and valuable men, for a cross between the gentry and the folk is often superior to the average of either; it has also saved the lower levels from a reversion to savagery. I have spoken so far of adultery in women. In men it is nowhere taken too seriously. Even the Catholic Church makes a clear distinction here.

10

I SELDOM if ever regret doing anything, even although I may be convinced that it was wrong. Once it is accomplished, I dismiss it from my mind.

11

IT IS rare indeed to find an actor who is a bachelor. The moment he is off with one wife he is on with another. He rushes from the bed to the altar almost as fast as other men rush from the altar to the bed.

12

OF ALL learned men, the clergy show the lowest development of professional ethics. Any pastor is free to cadge customers from the divines of rival sects, and to denounce the divines themselves as theological quacks. A large part of his professional activity, in fact, is given over to these enterprises. Doings that would cause a lawyer to be disbarred, a medical man to lose his license to practise, and even a chiropractor, a bartender or a whore-madam to be regarded as grossly unethical are part of his daily routine, and his admirers accept them as proofs of his consecration to holy works.

13

HAECKEL's recapitulation theory, if it is sound at all, apparently applies to mind as well as to body. That is to say, the mental history of the individual rehearses the mental evolution of the race. A new born baby is intellectually on all fours with a puppy, but the human mind begins to evolve on lines of its own at a very early age, and by the time a child is two years old it is plainly much more intelligent than any of the lower animals. This evolution goes on in the normal individual until the full mental powers of an adult are attained. Unfortunately, it is arrested in many cases, and so we have the great class of morons. Even in persons who are not absolutely morons, there may be arrests in this or that field. I have often argued that a poet more than thirty years old is simply an overgrown child. I begin to suspect that there may be some truth in it. Certainly the kind of mind that shows the easy credulity and disorderly enthusiasms of adolescence often survives into maturity, and even into old age.

The capacity to think at all is relatively recent. In all probability, it didn't develop, at least in its present form, until the beginning of the Stone Age. It is therefore not surprising to find many individuals in whom it has not reached its full development. In all of us the capacity to think is exercised somewhat clumsily, and only at relatively rare intervals. No human being can continue on the higher planes of thought for any great length of time. He is bound to go back, if only for relief, to more primitive patterns. The scholar turns to golf and the artist to drink. I have sat in in my time on what might plausibly be described as relatively profound discussions. I have noticed that their profundity was a matter of occasional flashes. Most of the time the debate went on on much lower levels. The great majority of human beings are probably quite incapable of ever operating on the higher levels of the superior man. Indeed, it may be said with some confidence that the average man never really thinks from end to end of his life. There are moments when his cogitations are relatively more respectable than usual, but even at their climaxes they never reach anything properly describable as the level of serious thought. The mental activity of such people is only a mouthing of clichés. What they mistake for thought is simply repetition of what they have heard. My guess is that well over eighty per cent. of the human race goes through life without ever having a single original thought. That is to say, they never think anything that has not been thought before and by thousands.

A society made up of individuals who were all capable of original thought would probably be unendurable. The pressure of ideas would simply drive it frantic. The normal human society is very little troubled by them. Whenever a new one appears the average man shows signs of dismay and resentment. The only way he can take in such a new idea is by translating it crudely into terms of more familiar ideas. That translation is one of the chief functions of politicians, not to mention journalists. They devote themselves largely to debasing the ideas launched by their betters. This debasement is intellectually reprehensible, but it is probably necessary to carry on the business of the world.

14

HUMAN life is basically a comedy. Even its tragedies often seem comic to the spectator, and not infrequently they actually have comic touches to the victim. Happiness probably consists largely in the capacity to detect and relish them. A man who can laugh, if only at himself, is never really miserable.

15

THE OBJECTION to a Communist always resolves itself into the fact that he is not a gentleman. It is not possible to engage in controversy with him as one engages in controversy with other men. He invariably hits below the belt if he can; indeed, his resentment is not so much against the economic structure of society as against its decorums. These decorums are mainly very ancient, and some of them are found even among savages. But the Communist always violates them.

16

THE STANDARDS of sexual ethics that prevail in so-called Christian countries are far too rigid to be workable. They seek to apply the same tests to all conduct below the belt, regardless of the personality of the individual and the circumstances of his or her life. To be sure, practical necessity forces a relaxation of this pedantry, but nevertheless it exists. Obviously, the same degree of conformity cannot be asked of all individuals without exception. A movie girl in Hollywood, making a large income and living otherwise like a medieval princess, certainly can't be asked to stick to the puritanical standards of conduct enforceable against a poor old maid in a country town. Even though her business keeps her under constant espionage, she is granted perforce a great measure of liberty. It is a sound human instinct which allows the rich a wider latitude than the poor. The damage to the rich is always less when they step aside from the standard. It is obviously no considerable calamity to a rich girl to lose her virtue, whereas it may be disaster of the first magnitude to a poor girl.

17

THE THING constantly overlooked by those hopefuls who talk of abolishing war is that it is by no means an evidence of decay but rather a proof of health and vigor. To fight seems to be as natural to man as to eat. Civilization limits and wars upon the impulse but it can never quite eliminate it. Whenever the effort seems to be most successful—that is, whenever man seems to be submitting most willingly to discipline, the spark is nearest to the powder barrel. Here repression achieves its inevitable work. The most warlike people under civilization are precisely those who submit most docilely to the rigid inhibitions of peace. Once they break through the bounds of their repressed but steadily accumulating pugnacity, their destructiveness runs to great lengths. Throwing off the chains of order, they leap into the air and kick their legs. Of all the nations engaged in the two World Wars the Germans, who were the most rigidly girded by conceptions of renunciation and duty, showed the most gusto for war for its own sake.

The powerful emotional stimulus of war, its evocation of motives and ideals which, whatever their error, are at least more stimulating than those which impel a man to get and keep a safe job—this is too obvious to need laboring. The effect on the individual soldier of its very horror, filling him with a sense of the heroic, increases enormously his self-respect. This increase in self-respect reacts upon the nation, and tends to save it from the deteriorating effects of industrial discipline. In the main, soldiers are men of humble position and talents—laborers, petty mechanics, young fellows without definite occupation. Yet no one can deny that the veteran shows a certain superiority in dignity to the average man of his age and experience. He has played his part in significant events; he has been a citizen in a far more profound sense than any mere workman can ever be. The effects of all this are plainly seen in his bearing and his whole attitude of mind. War may make a fool of man, but it by no means degrades him; on the contrary, it tends to exalt him, and its net effects are much like those of motherhood on women.

That war is a natural revolt against the necessary but extremely irksome discipline of civilization is shown by the difficulty with which men on returning from it re-adapt themselves to a round of petty duties and responsibilities.

This was notably apparent after the Civil War. It took three or four years for the young men engaged in that conflict to steel themselves to the depressing routine of everyday endeavor. Many of them, in fact, found it quite impossible. They could not go back to shovelling coal or tending a machine without intolerable pain. Such men flocked to the West, where adventure still awaited them and discipline was still slack. In the same way, after the Franco-Prussian War, thousands of young German veterans came to the United States, which seemed to them one vast Wild West. True enough, they soon found that discipline was necessary here as well as at home, but it was a slacker discipline and they themselves exaggerated its slackness in their imagination. At all events, it had the charm of the unaccustomed.

We commonly look upon the discipline of war as vastly more rigid than any discipline necessary in time of peace, but this is an error. The strictest military discipline imaginable is still looser than that prevailing in the average assembly-line. The soldier, at worst, is still able to exercise the highest conceivable functions of freedom—that is, he is permitted to steal and to kill. No discipline prevailing in peace gives him anything even remotely resembling this. He is, in war, in the position of a free adult; in peace he is almost always in the position of a child. In war all things are excused by success, even violations of discipline. In peace, speaking generally, success is inconceivable except as a function of discipline.

18

CANON law is much more rational than the civil law, and shows a far better understanding of psychology. Whenever it enacts a new statute provision is made for suspending that statute in appropriate cases, and an authority is set up for determining the conditions and beneficiaries of that suspension. So far as I am aware there is no article in the Catholic code that is applicable to everyone at all times and everywhere. Articles of minor importance may be suspended by such inferior authorities as confessors, but the suspension of more important ones is reserved to bishops and archbishops, or to the Pope. The Pope may waive even the prohibition against such serious crimes as murder, adultery, bigamy and blasphemy. Moreover, canon law is more succinct, and hence more understandable than the civil law, for it confines itself, in the main, to general provisions, and does not undertake to determine the minutiae of good and bad conduct. All such details are left to the discretion of the constituted authorities, who are oriental cadis rather than Western judges. Civil law would be much more rational, and what is better, much more effective, if it adopted this programme. As things stand, it is so complicated that not even lawyers can fathom it, and so arbitrary that it is constantly colliding with human nature.

19

ALL MORAL systems are grounded in the last analysis upon a scale of values. It is what men esteem that determines their conduct. Unfortunately, the values set up by the Christian system are largely false ones, and many of them are palpably so. They had worth to the primitive peoples among whom they arose, but their worth to modern man is sometimes zero. In fact, some of them are plainly not only worthless, but also dangerous—indeed, a few verge upon the suicidal. Mankind, to be sure, has learned to get around them in daily conduct, but nevertheless they are still whooped up by moral authority. Their survival is responsible for a large part of the moral uncertainty now prevailing. Every bright young man quickly learns that the moral mandates he is taught by his official elders are largely nonsensical. It is impossible to defend them in logic, and he can't help observing that many of them are not followed in practise. Nothing is more likely to promote what is commonly called immorality than the discovery that fundamental moral values are false.

20

MAN IS a beautiful machine that works very badly. He is like a watch of which the most that can be said is that its cosmetic effect is good.

21

No MAN of honor ever quite lives up to his code, any more than a moral man manages to avoid sin. If there were a confessional among men of honor analogous to that of the Catholic Church, its patrons would always have something to confess. They do things behind the door that they'd blush to death to acknowledge in public. Even that special kind of honor which is women's is compromised a bit by the hazards and exigencies of practical life, and no imaginable woman is adamant to the right combination of time, place and man. No one can ever really avoid what he holds to be evil. The Catholic is fortunate in the fact that the sinner can go to a priest and get rid of his sense of guilt. The Holy Ghost and the Holy Saints take over at least a part of his burden. But he, too, has to pay some penalty. Part of that penalty is that he is capable of committing sins, invented by the priest, which the unbeliever escapes altogether.

22

THE MAIN gain of modern man has been the weakening of governments. Unfortunately, that process is now reversed, not only in Europe, but also in America. There is a constant accession of governmental authority and power. It works inevitably toward the disadvantage of the only sort of man who is really worth hell room, to wit, the man who practises some useful trade in a competent manner, makes a decent living at it, pays his own way, and asks only to be let alone. He is now a pariah in all so-called civilized countries.

23

THE FACT that the pious Christian believes he will live forever is no proof that he will, though it is frequently cited as one. Even if all men believed it it would still not be true— and perhaps for that reason alone. All its persistence proves is that the majority of men are unable to grasp the concept of annihilation. They grasp readily enough the idea of being unconscious for a short time, but they are quite unable to think of being unconscious forever.

2 4

THE ART of writing, like the art of love, runs all the way from a kind of routine hard to distinguish from piling bricks to a kind of frenzy closely related to delirium tremens. Nearly all the whole of everyday journalism belongs to the former category: it is, in its customary aspects, no more than the reduction of vivid and recent impressions to banal sequences of time-worn words and phrases. The material all comes in from outside, and the writer has done well enough when he has turned it into a series of familiar rubber-stamps, instantly recognized by the generality of dolts, though not always understood. Even the art of editorial writing, which is to say, the formulation and statement of a gloss upon obvious facts, makes hardly any demand upon the psyche. The editorial writer, in his ordinary incarnation, simply translates banal and usually borrowed ideas into conventional phrases, as well settled by usage as those of a deed to real estate. Take away this outfit of rubber-stamps, and he is over his depth, and making heavy weather of it. No one ever heard of him saying anything really new: it would puzzle and irritate his customers. So with the generality of fiction writers. Their writing consists principally of a deft use of the familiar, the obvious. They may fetch up, on occasion, more or less novel ideas, but they almost always set them forth in a stereotyped way, and so leave them quite unadorned by novel aspects and original phrasing. All fiction save the occasional work of genius reads pretty much alike, and is couched in the same time-worn phrases. So is all writing of any other sort.

But consider the case of a man sitting down to write something genuinely original—to pump an orderly flow of ideas out of the turbid pool of his impressions, feelings, vague thoughts, dimly sensed instincts. He works in a room alone. Every jangle of the telephone cuts him like a knife; every entrance of a visitor blows him up. Solitary, lonely, tired of himself, wrought up to an abnormal sensitiveness, he wrestles abominably with intolerable complexities— shadowy notions that refuse to reveal themselves clearly, doubts that torture, hesitations that damn. His every physical sensation is enormously magnified. A cold in the head rides him like a witch. A split fingernail hurts worse than a laparotomy. The smart of a too-close shave burns like a prairie-fire. A typewriter that bucks is worse than a band of music. The far-away wail of a child is the howling of a fiend. A rattling radiator is a battery of artillery.

Nothing could be worse than this agony. A few hours of it and even the strongest man is thoroughly tired out. Days upon days of it, and he is ready for the doctor. The layman whose writing is confined to a few dozen letters a day can have no conceptions of the hard work done by such a writer. Worse, he must plod his way through many days when writing is impossible altogether—days of doldrums, of dead centers, of utter mental collapse. These days have a happy habit of coming precisely when they are most inconvenient—when a book has been promised and the publisher is snorting for it. They are days of unmitigated horror. The writer labors like a galley-slave, and accomplishes absolutely nothing. A week of such effort and he is a wreck. It is in the last ghastly hours of such weeks that writers throw their children out of sixth-story windows and cut off the heads of their wives.

But in the long run there is one consolation for this unhappy man of the pen. His feelings torture him far more than any other man is tortured, but soon or late he is able to work them off. They escape by way of his writings. Into those writings, if he lives long enough, he gradually empties all his fears and hatreds and prejudices—all his vain regrets and broken hopes—all his sufferings as a man, and all the special sufferings that go with his trade. The world, to such a man, never grows downright unbearable. There is always a sheet of paper. There is always a pen. There is always a way out.

25

THE ESSENTIAL difficulty of pedagogy lies in the impossibility of inducing a sufficiency of superior men and women to become pedagogues. Children, and especially boys, have sharp eyes for the weaknesses of the adults set over them. It is impossible to make boys take seriously the teaching of men they hold in contempt.

26

THE DIFFERENCE between a gentleman and a bounder is the difference between a duel and a fight in a barroom. In the latter the contestants yell while they are fighting, and gloat horribly in victory. The duelist fights without heat, and offers his hand to his fallen antagonist. This is pretty much the difference, too, between civilized war and the kind of war that is carried on by democratic countries. The latter is always accompanied by a tremendous amount of moral indignation.

2 7

IN ORDINARY human intercourse decorums are plainly more valuable than morals. No one really cares what the private morals of the other fellow may be, but there must be some confidence that he will react in ordinary situations according to the familiar patterns and without too much aberration. To take an interest in his private morals is, in fact, the sign of low culture. It is encountered only in primitive societies, such as those that are to be found in remote country towns. But even in the best society his manners are immensely important. No man can be really friendly to another whose personal habits differ materially from his own. Even the trivialities of table manners thus become important. The fact probably explains much of race prejudice, and even more of national prejudice. No American is ever really quite comfortable in the presence of an Englishman. The Englishman is cocksure in regions wherein the American is naturally diffident, and reserved in regions wherein the American is accustomed to be frank. The two men wear their clothes differently, devour their food according to different technics, and react differently to many other common situations. Each can become accustomed to the ways of the other, but it takes time, and in certain fields it takes a good deal of time.

Immigrants who live in this country for many years are still sharply conscious of the fact that it is a foreign land. It is only the native-born second generation that ever finds it really comfortable. I believe the same is true of Americans living abroad. I have met a great many of them in my time, and I can't recall a single one who was really happy. They are all pathetically eager to hear what is going on at home, especially those who pretend to be disgusted by American life.

28

ALL POETRY is simply an escape from reality. It says what is palpably not true. The only difference between poets is a difference in the kind of escape they crave. Some are content with visions of a pretty girl who is also a good cook and pays for the marketing out of her own funds; others demand the insane consolations of metaphysics, or the hiding-place of a jargon no one can understand.

29

THE NOTION that anything useful is accomplished by providing a large amount of leisure for the inferior man is probably full of folly. He invariably spends it foolishly. The five-day week is humane, and all rational men have supported it, but it would be silly to say that it has produced any public value, save the lowly value of making idiots happy. The beneficiary has enjoyed it subjectively, but only in his own imbecile way: it has given him more time to listen to the radio and look at movies. There is no sign whatever that any considerable number of the underprivileged have put their new leisure to really profitable use. They are just as stupid as they were before they had it; indeed, there is some reason to believe that they are more stupid.

3 0

IT MUST be confessed that man's inhumanity to man is almost intolerably distressing. It is the thing that all decent people chiefly complain against in this world. I have certainly done enough such complaining myself. Unfortunately, no workable cure for it has ever been discovered. It seems to be inevitable for all men, after they are put in position of authority, to exercise it in a brutal and inequitable manner. There is little choice here between one man and another, but if any difference can be demonstrated it probably stands to the credit of what are generally regarded as immoral men. The moral bully is the worst of all. Puritanism is completely merciless.

3 1

As SOON as any Negro becomes rich enough to be important to bankers and the Internal Revenue Bureau, he will live in a good part of Long Island and have a reserved table in the best restaurant in New York. Two-thirds of the social disabilities of the poor blackamoors, even in the South, are due to their economic inferiority.

3 2

THE TASTE for gambling, like that for sports, is a kind of feeble-mindedness—maybe even an insanity. It can be justified only by a resort to the most preposterous sophistry. Whenever it has seized a man of any visible talent—for example, Dostoevsky and C. C. Colton—he has ended crazy. It is the silliest of all the vices.

33

No GOVERNMENT is ever really in favor of so-called civil rights. It always tries to whittle them down. They are preserved under all governments, in so far as they survive at all, by special classes of fanatics, often highly dubious. The Hon. Frank Murphy, in his days as Attorney-General, announced with a flourish that he was setting up a bureau to guard civil rights, but that bureau, once it began to function, protected only the rights of those who favored the government. Its enemies remained *ferae naturae*.

34

WHY DO men delight in work? Fundamentally, I suppose, because there is a sense of relief and pleasure in getting something done—a kind of satisfaction not unlike that which a hen enjoys on laying an egg. Also, work offers an escape from boredom—a curse not only to men, but also to most of the other higher animals. There is nothing harder to do than nothing.

35

GOD IS the immemorial refuge of the incompetent, the helpless, the miserable. They find not only sanctuary in His arms, but also a kind of superiority, soothing to their macerated egos: He will set them above their betters. The same consolation for otherwise hopeless men is to be found in the concepts of King, President and so on. Such puissant creatures always attract and fascinate the third-rate. It is only an occasional Washington correspondent who can resist the

President's arm about his neck, the presidential scratch along his back. The favor of such magnificoes gives the inferior man a thrilling sense of importance, of power.

3 6

EQUALITY before the law is probably forever inattainable. It is a noble ideal, but it can never be realized, for what men value in this world is not rights but privileges. That fact is shown plainly in Russia. The rights that men have in common there are nextdoor to nil. What is sought and valued is a series of privileges that goes to persons who are faithful to the existing régime. They get the best jobs, the best dwellings, and all the favors that the government has at its disposal—indeed, the Russian system is almost exclusively a system of favors, and hence of privilege. People are kept in line for the administration by a series of rewards and punishments. The residium of inalienable rights is almost invisible.

This fact will probably work, in the long run, against the success of vertical unions in the United States. The skilled man always resents being put on a level with his inferiors. The craft unions are simply guilds set up to give their members exclusive privileges. It is impossible to imagine a really competent tool-maker consenting to have his welfare discussed and determined by sweepers. What happens when any such thing is attempted is also shown in Russia. Sweepers and tool-makers alike are divided into good party men and doubtful men, and the sweeper who is on the right side politically has advantages over the tool-maker who is not. The result must be a great deal of ill-feeling.

That ill-feeling probably explains the constant treachery that seems to go on in the Russian working units. A continuous investigation of it proceeds, and a great many culprits are unearthed.

The same thing began to show itself in the American vertical unions from the start. The more skilled men in the C.I.O. automobile union settled toward one side and the mere human mules toward the other. The battle over Communism was really, in all probability, a battle between these two factions. The idea that every working man, however incompetent, has certain inalienable craft rights can be maintained only by diminishing the rights of the really superior man. Thus the attempt to displace craft unions with vertical unions seems to be in for difficulties. It collides, like the Russian system, with certain irremovable facts of human nature. No man likes to be bossed by his inferiors. He is willing to take a certain amount of tyranny from his equals or superiors, but he resents the domination of those who know less than he does, and prove it daily by their inferior earning capacity. The effort of these inferiors is always to bring their earning capacity up, by artificial pressure, to that of better men. This can be done only by diminishing the earnings of the better men.

The Russians started out full of confidence that they could equalize incomes, but they quickly found that it was impossible. Soon there was as great a spread between the earnings of what is there regarded as a good man and those of the ordinary men as there is in any capitalist country— in fact, the spread in Russia was probably larger, for a superiority in wages there carried so many other privileges that figuring out the value of the whole becomes almost impossible. All that may be said with confidence is that the man who met the Russian test of merit—that is, one who was a faithful party hack—was compensated so much better than the skeptic that he appeared to belong to an altogether superior order of society.

3 7

FREE speech must either be thought of as a value in itself, or there is no use in thinking of it at all. Its exercise must inevitably benefit fools quite as much as sensible men, and in a democratic society the fools are almost sure to be sustained. Its utility lies in the fact that it enhances human dignity. In the case of the common run of men it sets up a kind of dignity that goes far beyond the deserts of those who pretend to it, but this must be endured in order to protect the genuine dignity of honest and intelligent men. All the rights and privileges of civilized man, under any democratic system, are similarly wasted upon worthless persons. The man who is barely human is treated as if he were the peer of Aristotle.

3 8

THE BASIC cause of the recurrent troubles in Europe is the fact that all the so-called countries are governed, under the prevailing system, by men who get and hold office by alarming the mob. Their principal business is the raising of bugaboos. Those bugaboos, at the start, are never believed in by rational men, but in the long run even rational men tend to succumb to the alarm. In the old days wars were pro-

duced by dynastic ambition. That motive is now in abey-
ance, but the thirst for power by demagogues is a quite
sufficient substitute for it.

39

THE UNITED STATES has not only failed to produce a genuine aristocracy; it has also failed to produce an indigenous
intelligentsia. The so-called intellectuals of the country are
simply weather-vanes blown constantly by foreign winds,
usually but not always English. When Stalin made his trade
with Hitler, in 1939 (now never mentioned by 100% Americans) two-thirds of the recognized native publicists were
caught, in Ben Stolberg's happy phrase, with their polemics
down. The New Deal fetched them by brigades, divisions
and army corps, and without wasting on them more than a
few rounds of blank cartridges. They were all ripe, in 1930,
for any sort of revelation, however bogus. The post-war
disillusion of the 1920's was simply too much for them to
bear. They were psychologically incapable of grasping the
concept of the irremediable. They believed as a cardinal
article of faith that there was a remedy at hand for every
conceivable public ill, just as the herbalists of the Middle
Ages believed that there was a cure in the fields or woods
for every disease of man. They were thus in a mood to
swallow any dose that quacks ventured to prescribe, and
were already half convinced before the New Dealers began to function. It was, indeed, instructive and at the same
time pathetic to see them leaping for every new remedy
recommended, even before the quacks had decided just
what it would cure. And when novelties began to run out,

they went back to all the exploded nostrums of the past, for example, the League of Nations. If anything was plain in 1930 it was that the League had been no more than a scheme of the English to consolidate their power in Europe: indeed, all the gloomiest forebodings of those who opposed it in 1920 had been borne out, and most abundantly. It was a fraud unmitigated, both in its purposes and in its effects. But in a little while all the American advanced thinkers were going back to it, and by 1935 they were arguing that relaunching it would put down war, bring peace and prosperity to the whole world, and inaugurate a reign of lovey-dovey. The effort here will be demonstrated abundantly in the course of time, and probably in a very short time, but the believing mind will not be convinced. On the contrary, it will begin to whoop up a third league to supplant the second, and then for a fourth to supplant the third, and so on. The same childish credulity is visible in the doctrine that the cure for the evils of democracy is more democracy. This is like saying that the cure for crime is more crime—the actual effect, though not the ostensible purpose, of the balderdash now preached by various groups of soaring criminologists.

Not many men can grasp the concept of the irremediable, or take in the fact that what happens in the world is only seldom modified by human volition. Most men even go beyond believing in volition; they actually hold that there is some mystical potency in mere faith. The resultant fallacies are innumerable, and only too painfully familiar. Uncle Julius has come down with cancer and the doctors have given him up; *ergo*, we must try chiropractic, or Christian

Science, or Swamproot, else we be accused (and, in our own eyes, convicted) of abandoning him to his doom. From this nonsense flows a very common corollary, to wit, that quack remedies must be somehow better than rational ones, since they at least promise to cure. The belief in such promises is the great curse of man. More than anything else, it impedes the progress of the race. Its chief beneficiaries are all enemies to mankind.

Historians will be diverted but certainly not edified by the bellowing of the American intelligentsia in the years following 1932. The effort some of them had made in the 1920's to view their country and the world with a realistic eye had left the whole corps exhausted, and, what is more, scandalized by their own temerity. They were thus ready to believe anything and everything, provided only that it was incredible. It would be flattery to say that they followed the Communist party line, though they undoubtedly made some effort to do so, hoping for light and leading. The Communist party line was really not enough for them; they also came out largely for a vast miscellany of other quackeries, and were presently so bogged in dogma that it was impossible for them to make themselves understood. They inhabit at all times what may be called a *limbus fatuorum*. Their imbecilities reveal dramatically the intellectual bankruptcy of the United States. The old minority of relatively civilized and rational men has pretty well disappeared.

40

THE OPPOSITION to capital punishment is supported very effectively by the delay in executing it. The seven years' wait of Sacco and Vanzetti revolted the world. The whole process should be shortened, to bring crime and punishment close together. As things stand, the spread is so great that by the time a criminal comes to the chair the crime is forgotten and all we see is a poor fish making a tremendous (and sometimes even gallant) effort to save his life, with all sorts of shyster lawyers and do-gooders as assistant heroes.

41

Very little of the extraordinary progress of medicine during the past century is to be credited to the family doctor, though he is still the official hero of the craft. To be sure, a few family doctors have contributed something to it, but never as family doctors. The case of Robert Koch is typical. He grossly neglected his patients at Langenhagen, Rackwitz and Wollstein in order to experiment with bacilli in his wife's kitchen. The American medical men of today had better be wary about spending too much energy in defending the family doctor. He is, at best, an humble artisan, not an artist or scientist. The men they should really fight for is the research man. He is always at a disadvantage under democratic government. Indeed, he is at a disadvantage under any sort of government, including that of the Rockefeller Institute or the board of trustees of the Johns Hopkins Medical School. He is essentially a free lance, a rebel, and his greatest value lies less in enriching medicine with new ideas than in exposing and destroying the old ideas that family doctors cherish.

Whatever actual value survives in the family doctor will be destroyed by the state medicine now impending. It will reduce him to the estate of a petty jobholder, and at the same time fill him with the grandiose pretensions of a bureaucrat. Soon or late, and probably distressingly soon, he is bound to begin treating his patients in a cavalier manner. It will not be to his interest to deal with them intelligently, competently, laboriously, and his character as their friend will vanish into his character as a Dogberry. In the end, he will resort inevitably to wholesale quackery. This has already happened under the panel system in England, and the mortality returns show it. No panel doctor has ever contributed anything to the progress of medicine, and no panel doctor can really have any active interest in his patients. He is a medical man only in the sorry sense that a newspaper editorial writer is a publicist.

42

CONGRESS, as the grand inquest of the country, has enormous powers. It need not observe the rules of evidence, and there is nothing save its own will to delimit the extent of its inquiries. It was a congressional investigation that dealt the first heavy blow to Prohibition. Even carried on by fools, as was the case with the Dies committee, such an investigation often reveals facts of value. The English Parliament is a continuing committee of inquiry, and its chief power and influence lie in that fact. The English long ago discovered that all government is evil, and that the best way to endure it is to treat it as a suspicious character, watching it at every step. In the United States this scrutiny is less constant, and as a result the American government is more daring and presumptuous. A vigilant journalism might compensate for the pusillanimity of Congress here, but American journalism has long since ceased to be vigilant.

43

THE EFFORT to educate the uneducable is hopeless. Schools for adults soon become kindergartens for adults. The pupils are quite unable to take in the education proper to their years. The gogues thus have to provide them with amusement, just as children of four are provided with amusement in kindergartens. The hope is that they will somehow learn to think as an accidental by-product of playing, but that hope is vain.

44

ALL PROFESSIONAL philosophers tend to assume that common sense means the mental habit of the common man. Nothing could be further from the mark. The common man is chiefly to be distinguished by his plentiful *lack* of common sense: he believes things on evidence that is too scanty, or that distorts the plain facts, or that is full of non sequiturs. Common sense really involves making full use of *all* the demonstrable evidence—and of nothing *but* the demonstrable evidence.

45

THE SCIENTIST who yields anything to theology, however slight, is yielding to ignorance and false pretenses, and as certainly as if he granted that a horse-hair put into a bottle of water will turn into a snake.

46

WHY HAS no one ever written a treatise on sexual morals based upon the actual practises of civilized men? It would differ enormously from all the current texts on the subject. For one thing it would reject as completely absurd the doctrine that any act of sex outside marriage is immoral *per se*. No man of any sense believes this, or conducts his life on the theory that it is true. Yet he also has his inhibitions, and some of them are strong ones. They should be listed and investigated. One of them, it seems to me, is that any act of sex becomes dishonorable (*not,* it is to be noted, immoral) the instant it begins to imperil the dignity and security of the other party, or, indeed, of any other person. Apparently some such idea was at the bottom of the section on sexual offenses in the Code Napoléon. Nothing so enlightened is to be found in the code of England and the United States.

47

IN THE long years of my contact with American authors I have never known a single one of genuine skill who was not quickly recognized and appreciated. Dreiser, in the days after "Sister Carrie," had a large and influential body of advocates, and if he was unknown to Americans in general it was mainly because he wrote nothing for nine years after "Sister Carrie" was published. Once he printed "Jennie Gerhardt," even the newspapers became aware of him. Meanwhile, though he was writing nothing save a few short stories, he yet made a very good living. At the time he was editor of the *Delineator*, 1907–10, he received $10,000 a year. That was a really colossal salary in those days.

Whitman got quite enough to live on; in fact, he managed to accumulate an estate of at least $10,000. Ambrose Bierce, though he was supposed to be a neglected genius, actually received a salary of $100 a week from Hearst, and it kept on long after his writings ceased to have any newspaper value. So with all the other martyrs of the literary art. They are unanimously bogus. In the depths of the Depression all of those of my acquaintance still lived in reasonable comfort. There was, in fact, a continuing demand for good work, and the rewards offered were at least adequate.

Among the so-called writers assembled by the Federal Arts Project, I can't recall a single one of any genuine skill. I have heard that Harry Kemp was on the roll for a while, but Kemp by that time was played out, and could write nothing fit to print. Another typical dole-bird was Maxwell Bodenheim—a pure faker. He had been a failure all his life, and with sound reason, and in the end he went crazy and was finally murdered in 1954. All through the Depression I received frequent letters from editors beseeching me to find authors to do articles for them.

In my brief days as editor of the *Evening Sun*, in the Spring of 1938, I had a member of the staff investigate the thirty or forty so-called writers on the payroll of the Federal Writers' Project, Maryland Division. He found that only one of them claimed to be an actual writer, and that the name of that one could not be found in any of the standard reference books, not even in the very hospitable Read-

er's Guide to Periodical Literature. If he ever wrote anything for magazines, it must have been for the pulp variety.
The rest ranged from an Egyptian who had operated a news-
stand to a bartender, and included bookkeepers, salesmen,
insurance solicitors and a genealogist, but no authors. The
guide-book to Maryland produced by these frauds took
years in the making, and cost more than $200,000. In Au-
gust, 1938, there were 52 persons on the payroll and the
budget ran to $4200 a month. The first boss of the project
was a minor Johns Hopkins pedagogue named Karle Singe-
wald. He was demoted in 1939 or thereabout, and his place
given to Alexander M. Saunders, an obscure Johns Hopkins
tutor in English, never heard of afterward. The text was so
bad that Saunders had to rewrite it from A to izzard. His
own talents being meagre, he produced a very bad book.
How the fakers on the payroll were chosen I do not know,
but it was manifest that the Communists had a hand in the
business.

4 8

ONE OF the strangest delusions of the Western mind is to
the effect that a philosophy of profound wisdom is on tap
in the East. I have read a great many expositions of it, some
by native sages and the rest by Western enthusiasts, but I
have found nothing in it save nonsense. It is, fundamentally, a moony transcendentalism almost as absurd as that
of Emerson, Alcott and company. It bears no sort of relation to the known facts, and is full of assumptions and
hypotheses that every intelligent man must laugh at. In its
practical effects it seems to be as lacking in sense and as

inimical to human dignity as Methodism, or even Mormonism. The Hindus, save when they have been denaturized by Western influences, are actually barbarians, and this is true of the highest class of Brahmins as plainly as of the untouchables. Their ethical system is heavy with imbecile taboos—against perfectly sound and useful foods, against alcohol, against contraception, against common decency. According to Katherine Mayo ("Mother India," Volume II; New York, 1931) even the most "civilized" eminentissimos of the Hindu community believe that their souls are imperiled if their daughters do not marry at puberty. This grotesque superstition is responsible for some of the worst cruelties visible in the modern world. Only a few years ago I was reading about three child wives who had lost their lives because their pious husbands refused to allow them competent medical aid in childbirth. The most backward savages in Africa are not more vile.

The so-called philosophy of India is even more blowsy and senseless than the metaphysics of the West. It is at war with everything we know of the workings of the human mind, and with every sound idea formulated by mankind. If it prevailed in the whole modern world we'd still be in the Thirteenth Century; nay, we'd be back among the Egyptians of the pyramid age. Its only coherent contribution to Western thought has been theosophy—and theosophy is as idiotic as Christian Science. It has absolutely nothing to offer a civilized white man.

49

ONE OF the cavernous holes in Christianity is to be found
in the fact that the Creator it professes to serve and glorify
is only too obviously a great deal less intelligent, not to say
a great deal less decent, than the more honest and enlightened varieties of man. His moral system, as it is ex-
pounded in the two Testaments, is certainly neither as
rational nor as ennobling as some of the moral systems devised by human beings. Even savages, in this department,
often surpass Him. Nor does He show any of the intellectual qualities that we associate with the superior sort of
man, for He lavishes enormous means on mean ends, He
appears to be quite lacking in ordinary forethought, and
many of His most elaborate devices fail of the effect apparently intended. An ordinary mechanic who showed such
incompetence would be discharged quickly; a scientist so
stupid would be classed with phrenologists and chiropractors, perhaps even with pedagogues and psychiatrists. The
problem of evil simply refuses to be solved. There are massive proofs, even in everyday life, that the God of Christianity cannot be a beneficent Being, but must be predominantly maleficent. In the ages of faith—which extended into
our own time—the fact that He had apparently invented
disease was disposed of by the theory that He had also created a remedy for every malady. But no one of any intelligence believes this today, for the fact is too plain that there
was no genuine progress in the cure of disease until man
began inventing remedies of his own, not occurring in nature. To be sure, he still makes use of remedies that do so

occur, but every year they tend to be fewer, relatively speaking. In the end, perhaps, they will fall out of use altogether, and man will combat illness, as he already combats distance, with devices wholly of his own devising.

50

THE EXISTENCE of most human beings is of absolutely no significance to history or to human progress. They live and die as anonymously and as nearly uselessly as so many bullfrogs or houseflies. They are, at best, undifferentiated slaves upon an endless assembly line, and at worst they are robots who leave their mark upon time only by occasionally falling into the machinery, and so incommoding their betters. The familiar contention that they at least have some hand in *maintaining* civilization—that if they do nothing to promote it they at all events do not retard it—this contention is plainly not valid. If all human beings were like them civilization would not be maintained at all: it would go back steadily, and perhaps quickly. This is proved by a glance at Appalachia, the domain of "the only pure Anglo-Saxons" left in the United States. The culture prevailing among these backward folk is precisely the same today as it was when the great movement into the West began, and they were thrown off from the stream of more intelligent and enterprising pioneers. Save for the infiltration of a few cultural traits from outside, they live now exactly as their ancestors lived then. They eat the same food, maintain the same societal patterns, entertain the same ideas, and tremble before the same barbaric god. If they have yielded to improvement in this or that particular, it has always been against their will and in spite of their resistance. In so far as they have initiated any change themselves, that change has been retrogressive. They are relatively much less civilized today than they were when their flight to the highlands began, and in many particulars they are also less civilized absolutely.

The torch of civilization is carried, not by such miserable nonentities, but by a small minority of more restless and enterprising men. The members of this minority work in countless ways, and there is an immense variation in the nature and value of their several activities, but all such activities tend in the same direction. What they always aim at, whether by design or only instinctively, is the improvement of human life on this earth. They strive to make it more rational, more secure, more abundant. One of them may do no more than devise a new and better rat-trap, or a new way to make beans, or a new phrase, but some other, on some near tomorrow, may synthesize edible proteins or square the circle. Out of this class come not only all the men who enrich civilization, but also all those who safeguard it. They are the guardians of what it has gained in the past as well as the begetters of all it gains today and will gain hereafter. Left to the great herd it would deteriorate inevitably, as it has deteriorated in the past whenever the supply of impatient and original men has fallen off. This is the true secret of the rise and fall of cultures. They rise so long as they produce a sufficiency of superior individuals, and they begin to fall the moment the average man approximates their best.

Here we have an easy and accurate gauge of nations.

Is their production of superior men above, equal to or below the mean? Do they contribute more or less than other nations to the general progress of civilization? Apply this test to any existing country or community, and you will be able to place it in the scale. Obviously enough, the position of such a group as the people of Appalachia is very near the bottom. For a century or more they have produced next to nothing that is of any genuine value to humanity. Virtually all their men of mark have been men of wholly factitious, and indeed of fictitious distinction—political demagogues, theological obscurantists, military bullies, and so on. They have not hatched a single man of science of any size, or a single artist above the level of a village poet, or a single innovator in manufacturing, trading or any other practical enterprise. They have even failed to produce a criminal of any genuine originality. Compare their record with that of any community of better quality, say the population of Massachusetts, or Ohio, or Wisconsin, or even Delaware or Rhode Island, and you will begin to realize the gap that separates civilized man from his camp-followers and parasites. If all the inhabitants of the Appalachian chain succumbed to some sudden pestilence tomorrow, the effect upon civilization would be but little more than that of the fall of a meteor into the Ross Sea or the jungles of the Amazon.

The application of this test produces results that are sharply at variance with what is taught by popular soothsayers and generally believed. Put to it, Japan, for example, takes a very high place in the scale, falling only a little below that of the most cultured nations of the West. It rises almost immeasurably above any other oriental nation. China and India live mainly in the past, and have given the world little or nothing of sound value for centuries. They fail not only generally, but also in every particular. They have contributed nothing for many years to either the arts or the sciences, and even less to the practical business of living. Their political ideas are crude and irrational, and they produce no valuable goods save raw materials. Japan, on all these counts, is enormously their superior. Though it came into the orbit of Western civilization much later than they did, or indeed than any other oriental nation did, it has forged far ahead of them in a few generations, and is now quite fit to be measured with England, France, Germany or the United States. Its scientists, its men of business and even its artists pull their full weight in the boat. In free competition with the West it began to show a high degree of capacity and originality back in the 80's, and during the years before World War II it was making progress as fast as any other nation, and faster than most— as its extraordinary successes against British shipping and manufactures showed. Up to the turn of the century it was an importer of both goods and ideas, but after World War I it began to export both. There is hardly a science in which Japanese names do not shine, and there is not a form of practical enterprise.

The appearance of a new nation in the first rank causes painful concern among those already there, and history shows that efforts are always made to put it down. The entrance of Germany was the primary cause of World War I, and the attempt to reduce it to subjection and inferiority after it lost the war was one of the two principal causes of World War II. The other cause, of course, was the rise of Japan. In both cases England was the nation mainly aggrieved and alarmed, and in both cases it was seconded by the United States. These nations, at the beginning of the Nineteenth Century, seemed to be safely dominant in the world, and indeed their domination was assumed as a sort of axiom. When it began to be challenged there were two courses open to them. One was to bestir themselves sufficiently to regain their vanishing primacy; the other was to try to destroy their rivals. The first course was made difficult and perhaps impossible by the fact that both were heavily burdened by a proletariat that had gained political power, and was firmly against the devices needed to make them formidable competitors. They still had minorities of highly civilized and competent individuals, but those minorities were hobbled by the inertia of the masses and denied escape by the political hegemony of the masses. They were thus forced to resort to the second of the two courses I have mentioned. That is to say, they were forced to try to destroy by arms the two nations that had risen to rivalry with them, and were unburdened in competition, as they were, by powerful resistance from below.

It is not likely that the two World Wars will solve the problem. There has been great slaughter on both sides, but it has been chiefly among the robots. There has also been an enormous destruction of property, but it has been mainly either of things that can be quickly replaced or of things of more sentimental than practical value. Indeed, there is some ground for arguing that the destruction has been beneficial rather than otherwise, for it becomes manifest that the United States, which escaped unscathed from both wars, will have to destroy deliberately much of the sort of property that was destroyed in Europe and Asia by military vandalism. In other words, its plants will need modernizing to meet the competition of the new plants built to replace the war's ruins.

5 1

THE AVERAGE American college fails doubly to achieve its ostensible ends. One failure, I believe, flows from its apparent inability to find out precisely what a given student, A, is fitted by nature to learn, and what sort of learning will yield him the most benefit, considering his congenital capacities and environmental background. Anything else that he is taught is wasted. It may give him a certain superficial appearance of improvement, but that improvement will be useless alike to himself and to the world. The second failure of the colleges lies in their apparent incompetence to select and train a sufficient body of intelligent teachers. Their choice is commonly limited to second-raters, for a man who really knows a subject is seldom content to spend his lifetime teaching it: he wants to function in a more active and satisfying way, as all other living organisms want to function. There are, of course, occasional exceptions to this rule, but they are very rare, and none of them are to be found in the average college. The pedagogues there incarcerated are all inferior men—men who really know very little about the things they pretend to teach, and are too stupid or too indolent to acquire more.

Being taught by them is roughly like being dosed in illness by third-year medical students.

52

THE NAME of Beethoven is probably unknown to nine Americans out of ten, and so is that of Schubert. Yet these men, both long dead, still manage to present their ideas to the American people. To be sure, the average Americano could not stand their music undiluted, but as it has been stolen and puffed up by jazz performers he swallows it greedily. A great composer really cuts a wider swath than any other kind of artist. Even a second-rater such as Mendelssohn probably impinges upon the consciousness of the average man or woman far more than Shakespeare.

53

THE ADVANCE of science is accompanied by a corresponding advance in quackery. The sciences are far too difficult to be grasped, even in principle, by the overwhelming majority of human beings. Consider, for example, the case of an ignorant patient confronted by pathology. There is simply no way for his physician to tell him just what is the matter with him, for all the concepts on which the explanation must be based, and even most of its terms, are incomprehensible to him. A very substantial training in anatomy, physiology, histology, bacteriology and various other complex disciplines is necessary to their understanding. Thus the patient, sweating for an idea of what ails him, becomes an easy mark for the nearest chiropractor, who shows him a crude chart on the wall, and tells him glibly that all disease is caused by the pressure of the vertebral bones upon the nerves issuing from the vertebral foramina. This is not true, but it appears to be supported by the chiropractor's chart, and it is at least simple and hence understandable to even the meanest understanding. So the patient succumbs readily, as stupid men always succumb to facile and foolish explanations, and presently he is dead of the disease that the educated physician could not make him comprehend. The more complicated pathology becomes, the easier it is to repeat this process.

Science has another and even more dubious rival in metaphysics, which operates on a higher level. Its recurrent resurrections are all based on the fact that many presumably educated men are quite incapable of grasping scientific concepts. The business is too laborious for them, too troublesome. They thus seek answers to their questions in much smoother waters. In other words, they seek them in speculation, not in experiment and study. Sitting in a comfortable library, they are able to frame answers in a few hours that scientists find impossible after long years of hard work. Their subsequent efforts to clothe these answers in pompous words, to make them seem recondite and portentous, are only afterthoughts. The essential part is always quite simple. It is nothing more or less than a silly denial that facts are important. As commonly encountered, it takes the form of the doctrine that materialism is somehow sordid, and even more or less immoral. Yet it is materialism, operating on the plane of common sense, that has brought the human race all the progress it has seen in five hundred years. Metaphysics has contributed precisely nothing to the process; on the contrary, it has been an impediment. Medicine never really got anywhere until it threw metaphysics overboard. Find me a medical man who still toys with it, and I'll show you a quack. He may be, perhaps, what is called an ethical quack, but still he is a quack.

54

MEN ALWAYS try to make virtues of their weaknesses. Fear of death and fear of life both become piety.

55

THE WORLD presents itself to me, not chiefly as a complex of visual sensations, but as a complex of aural sensations. The fact explains many of my prejudices and weaknesses— for example, my defective appreciation of painting. It explains something a good deal more elusive: my taste in women. I seldom give much heed to the faces and forms of females, and I almost never notice their clothes. But when one of them has a low-pitched and soft voice, with a good clang-tint, she is free to consume my wealth and waste my time whenever the spirit moves her.

56

AMERICAN law has made very little real progress since the days of Blackstone. In large part it still belongs to the Fifteenth Century. There has been some effort to get rid of its worst absurdities in England, but hardly any in the United States. If medicine had remained as backward the doctors would still believe in the humoral pathology, and their chief remedial agent would be blood-letting.

57

Philosophy consists very largely of one philosopher arguing that all others are jackasses. He usually proves it, and I should add that he also usually proves that he is one himself.

58

When a new idea appears in the world and it turns out on investigation to be more or less sound, mankind is never content to leave it so. There is an apparent inevitable tendency to enmesh it in bosh. Some of the ideas in Socialism are surely not insane: they are grounded upon accurate observation and developed by common sense. But the Marxians have never been content to let them alone. Bit by bit they have been swathed in puerile speculation, until some of the best of them are now almost unintelligible. The so-called Marxian dialectic is simply an effort by third-rate men to give an air of profundity to balderdash. Christianity has gone the same way. There are some sound ideas in it, but its advocates always add a lot of preposterous nonsense. The result is theology.

59

I live in a town which also houses an archbishop. Not infrequently I meditate in wonder upon his awful powers. They are seldom mentioned by his fellow citizens, yet they exist all the while. He can bind and loose alike in Heaven and on this earth; he can dispense from all the consequences of sin, whether natural or revealed; he can do many other extraordinary things. His subordinates are in many cases charming fellows, and it is pleasant to meet them at the *Biertisch*; nevertheless, they remain magicians as he is, and believe in all sincerity that they can perform feats enormously more difficult than those of Merlin. The survival of such fantastic characters in modern society is all the proof we need that civilization is still only a superficial dermatosis.

60

CAPITAL punishment has failed in America simply because it has never been tried. If all criminals of a plainly incurable sort were put to death tomorrow there would be enormously less crime in the next generation. England tried that scheme in the Eighteenth Century, and with great success. To be sure, a great many persons were killed who were no worse than weaklings succumbing in the face of irresistible temptation, but it is not to be forgotten that the genuinely criminal were stamped out along with the weaklings. As a result England shows a low crime rate today. The tendency to crime, call it whatever you will, has been pretty well obliterated. For one Englishman who in the face of severe temptation or provocation is moved to homicide, you will find ten Frenchmen and probably a hundred Americans. The Englishman has been bred to resist such temptations as dogs have been bred to eschew leaping on the table at dinner time and grabbing the food. He may not be superior to the less natural man, but he at least makes a more comfortable neighbor. Compare him, at his worst, to a Mississippian or a Texan.

61

THE NOTION that a man who <u>rejects the current scheme,</u> whatever it is, is an immoral and abandoned fellow is pure delusion. He may be, in fact, an extraordinarily rigid purist, and far more straightlaced than a Quaker or a monk. No man of any intelligence whatever can escape the ethical problem, save perhaps by fleeing to a desert island. He may hold himself sniffishly aloof from the current certainties, but all the while he is bound by certainties of his own, partly arising from his heritage but probably in greater part from his environment. My own primary ethical maxim, I suspect, was borrowed from my father, whose moral system I have elsewhere described as predominantly Chinese. It is to the effect that it is inexcusably immoral to break engagements. This maxim carries me to curious lengths. I am, for one thing, constitutionally unable to owe money. An undischarged debt of ten dollars worries me beyond all reason. *Per corollary*, I greatly dislike persons who lack that squeamishness. Let a man get into my debt for money and not discharge the obligation promptly, and I am against him for life. Whatever his apparent merits otherwise, I dislike him and avoid him, and don't want his good will. Especially, I don't want to hear his excuses, however sound and pathetic: all I ask is that he take himself out of my sight, and stay there. The thing goes even further. I dislike intensely anyone who forgets appointments or is habitually late. When I say that I'll come to dinner at seven o'clock I am there at seven o'clock, though the heavens fall. When I agree to deliver a manuscript on a certain date, I deliver

it on or before that date. In all my life I have missed but
two trains—once in my schooldays, delayed by a too garru-
lous pedagogue, and once at sixty, delayed by the lateness
of another train. This prejudice often poisons my relations
with women, some of whom practise tardiness as an egoistic
indulgence, seeking to show their power to make men stand
and deliver. I have never stood and delivered to such a
wench more than once. All the women I know today, save
one, are prompt, and that one has an excuse in an extraordinarily dilatory husband. I tolerate her simply because I
believe she can't help herself. If she did not exist I'd never
see *him*.

6 2

In the field of practical morals popular judgments are often
sounder than those of the self-appointed experts. These
experts seldom show any talent for the art and mystery
they undertake to profess; on the contrary, nine-tenths of
them are obvious quacks. They are responsible for all the
idiotic moral reforms and innovations that come and go,
afflicting decent people. And they are the main, and often
the only advocates of moral ideas that have begun to wear
out, and deserve to be scrapped. The effort to put down
birth control, led by Catholic theologians but with a certain amount of support from Protestant colleagues, offers
a shining case in point. The more the heat is applied to
them, the more Catholic women seem to resort to the devices of the Devil, on sale in every drugstore. Many of these
women are genuinely pious, but into their piety there has
been introduced an unhappy doubt, perhaps only half formulated. It is a doubt about the professional competence of

their moral guides and commanders. They have not only begun to view the curious fiats of bishops and archbishops with a growing indifference; they have also begun to toy with the suspicion that even the Pope, on occasion, may be all wet. His first anathemas against contraception were plain and unqualified, but of late he has begun to hedge prudently, and it is now quite lawful for a Catholic woman to avoid pregnancy by a resort to mathematics, though she is still forbidden to resort to physics and chemistry. This concession is a significant admission that the original position of the moral theologians was untenable. In other words, it is an admission that they were wrong about a capital problem of their trade—and that the persons they sought to teach were right.

63

ONLY a country that is rich and safe can afford to be a democracy, for democracy is the most expensive and nefarious kind of government ever heard of on earth. The four volumes of Sandburg's Lincoln are full of shocking accounts of the corruption that went on during the Civil War.

64

THE NOTION that the object of punishment is to dissuade the criminal from his evil courses still seems to have some life in it. It is, of course, mainly a hollow sentimentality. Who ever heard of dissuading a Dillinger? The actual object of punishment is simply to get rid of the criminal. Society can't endure him, and so it tries to devise some scheme to dispose of him. The scheme of locking him up is obviously a failure. To be sure, it keeps him out of circulation while he is actually behind the bars, but there is little certainty that he will stay there, and meanwhile the cost of maintaining him is enormous. The easiest and cheapest way to deal with Dillingers is to kill them. If it be argued that this is mere revenge, the answer is plain: Why not? Revenge is certainly as sound an emotion as any other. Once a man has attacked another with arms he should be regarded as a criminal, and if he ever does it again he should be hanged forthwith, regardless of the immediate effect of his crime. The legal differentiation between shooting at a man and missing him and shooting at him and hitting him is completely absurd. The thing that should be punished is the impulse, not the technic. If we had 2,000 executions a year in the United States instead of 130, there would be an immense improvement. I don't think that many innocent men would be in danger. Every one knows who the principal professional criminals are. In Germany Hitler rounded them up and beheaded them at once. In order to make the thing legal he proclaimed a number of *ex post facto* laws. Such laws, of course, are forbidden by the national Constitution and most of the State constitutions. Nevertheless, there is nothing in these instruments forbidding hanging habitual criminals. After a man has spent two or three years in defiance of the law, raiding the property of others and endangering their lives, it is certainly absurd to proceed on the assumption that he is an injured innocent.

It would be shocking to have 2,000 executions in one year, but the shock would soon wear off, and we'd at least be rid of 2,000 criminals. The present system is so ineffective as to be idiotic. It is impossible to hang the average murderer until he has killed at least a dozen people. Meanwhile, his tendencies are notorious, and no rational man doubts that he will keep on killing so long as he is at liberty. Even if he is locked up, he goes on in the same way. Certainly there is no reason why such rogues should be permitted to menace the life of prison warders. Yet they do it constantly. They are always trying to escape, and everyone knows that they never hesitate to kill in order to make good their effort.

Unless we reject free will totally and in all departments, so that the good are no more honored and the wicked no more detested, we must admit its reality as a practical matter. Well, getting rid of criminals is a practical matter. If psychiatry could really cure them, every rational man would be for it, if only as an easy way to dispose of a nuisance. But so long as psychiatry remains mainly quackery we must contrive to get them into such a position that they can't do any further harm. The one certain, swift and cheap way to deal with them is to put them to death. The fact that criminality seems to normal men irrational is certainly no reason for sparing the criminal. There is, indeed, just as much logic in killing homicidal maniacs as there is in killing murderers who are plainly sane. The sane ones, at least in theory, may be on some theoretical tomorrow dissuaded, but the maniacs are admittedly hopeless. A really rational society would dispose of all such mental cripples humanely and at once. Their continued living is not only a source of danger to others, but a source of hopeless misery to themselves. If they could step out of their fogs momentarily most of them would choose death to the sort of lives they lead. In this field a maudlin and bogus humanitarianism does some of its worst work. Its obvious and certain effect is to augment the amount of misery in the world. It not only preserves people whose own lives are hideous; it also offers a constant menace to the lives and welfare of people who might otherwise live safely and at peace.

65

EVERY history written by a confessedly Catholic historian, say Hilaire Belloc, is shot through with palpable imbecilities. He starts out with such absurd prepossessions that it is quite impossible for him to tell his story honestly. The way to test the worth of Belloc's English history is to ask yourself what he would have to put into a history of the Church. Imagine his account of the medieval Popes—say, Alexander VI—and of the saints. To be sure, there have been Catholic historians who have admitted that Alexander was not altogether admirable, but all of them have swathed that admission in loud and disarming praises of his virtues, most of them imaginary. When a Catholic historian deals with the saints he is as ridiculously hobbled as a writer of American school histories dealing with the Mexican War, the Spanish-American War, or the first two World Wars. In order to account for them at all he must ascribe to them magical powers that had no actual existence, and are not believed in by any rational man. Indeed, he must write all of his history on the assumption that ordinary priests also have magical powers. Thus he is always a dubious character, professionally speaking. Even though he may unearth a great deal of valuable material, he is debarred from deal-

ing with it in a frank and free manner. He is forbidden to
deal realistically with most of the larger events and implications of his history, and must confine himself, if he would
be safe, to the puerilities of official chronology. Once he
begins to interpret the material he has amassed he is hobbled by his preconceived notions, all of them obviously unsound. I find it impossible to accept seriously the conclusions as to Cromwell or Charles I of a historian who is
bound to believe and say that the hallucinations of the
peasant girl of Lourdes were actually events.

66

WHEN war is defended upon the usual grounds, nearly always purely moralistic, it quickly becomes a palpable fraud.
No man of any intelligence or dignity could be imagined
carrying it on for the objects commonly stated. It degener-
ates to the level of a vice crusade. Perhaps it is never really
defensible save when it is thought of as its own sufficient
end.

67

THE CAPACITY of human beings to bore one another seems
to be vastly greater than that of any other animals. Some of
their most esteemed inventions have no other apparent
purpose, for example, the dinner party of more than two,
the epic poem, and the science of metaphysics.

68

IT SEEMS to be difficult if not impossible for human beings
to avoid thinking of government as a mystical entity with
a nature and a history all its own. It constitutes for them a

creature somehow interposed between themselves and the great flow of cosmic events, and they look to it to think for them and to protect them. In democratic countries it is theoretically their agent, but there seems to be a strong tendency to convert the presumably free citizen into its agent, or, at all events, its client. This exalted view of its scope, character, powers and autonomy is fundamentally false. A government, at bottom, is nothing more than a gang of men, and as a practical matter most of them are inferior men. Its business, in civilized countries, seldom attracts the service of really superior individuals: its eminentissimos are commonly nonentities who gain all their authority by belonging to it, and are of small importance otherwise. Yet these nonentities, by the intellectual laziness of men in general, have come to a degree of puissance in the world that is unchallenged by that of any other group. Their fiats, however preposterous, are generally obeyed as a matter of duty, they are assumed to have a kind of wisdom that is superior to ordinary wisdom, and the lives of multitudes are willingly sacrificed in their interest. Government is actually the worst failure of civilized man. There has never been a really good one, and even those that are most tolerable are arbitrary, cruel, grasping and unintelligent. Indeed, it would not be far wrong to describe the best as the common enemy of all decent citizens. But there will be small hope of gaining adherents to this idea so long as government is thought of as an independent and somehow super-human organism, with powers, rights and privileges transcending those of any other human aggregation.

69

RELIGIOUS people constantly make the mistake of assuming that the non-religious man is always actively hostile to the faith. This is certainly not true. The militant atheist, as a matter of fact, is commonly a man who is actually religious at bottom, and very often he ends his career on the bosom of Holy Church, or as a Christian Scientist. The average unbeliever simply does not care a damn. Religion amuses him faintly, as any other superstition amuses him, but it does not excite him. The number of such indifferent persons is much larger than is commonly assumed. They are not organized, and hence make no public pother, but they exist in immense hordes, and offer a steadily increasing menace to all forms of Christianity. It has little to fear from Communists and other such raucous enemies, for what they believe in is plainly quite as absurd as what Christians believe in. Active enmity, in fact, commonly prospers it. But disdain is something else again.

70

THE RUSSIAN proletarians who were to have been made rich, fat and happy by the triumph of the Marxian gospel are still eating herring and black bread and getting $7 cash a month, but their saviors are riding about in imported cars, sleeping with perfumed women and living in steam-heated flats. If it be true, as the American Communists allege, that 10% of the American people own 90% of the national wealth, then it is equally true that 5% of the Russians eat 95% of the caviare and drink 100% of the champagne.

71

THERE are people who read too much: the bibliobibuli. I know some who are constantly drunk on books, as other men are drunk on whiskey or religion. They wander through this most diverting and stimulating of worlds in a haze, seeing nothing and hearing nothing.

72

I AM willing to go along with any innovator so long as I am convinced that he is making a sincere effort to arrive at the truth. But the moment I begin to suspect that his desire for the truth is corrupted by an itch to sell something I quit him.

73

A COMPLETELY honest autobiography is probably impossible. It is imaginable, of course, that a given man may try to tell the whole truth about himself, at least as he remembers it and understands it; but in dealing with others even the most babbling sort of man is bound to respect a few confidences and a few conventions. I have, in my desultory reminiscences, both published and unpublished, dealt pretty freely with some of my contemporaries, but in no case have I told even so much as half of what I know about them, and the part I have told has always been the least embarrassing part.

74

ASTRONOMERS and physicists, dealing habitually with objects and quantities far beyond the reach of the senses, even with the aid of the most powerful aids that ingenuity has been able to devise, tend almost inevitably to fall into the ways of thinking of men dealing with objects and quantities that do not exist at all, *e.g.*, theologians and metaphysicians. Thus their speculations tend almost inevitably to depart from the field of true science, which is that of precise observation, and to become mere soaring in the empyrean. The process works backward, too. That is to say, their reports of what they pretend actually to *see* are often very unreliable. It is thus no wonder that, of all men of science, they are the most given to flirting with theology. Nor is it remarkable that, in the popular belief, most astronomers end by losing their minds.

75

THE ESSENTIAL stupidity of the New Deal, and of all other such massive quackeries, lies in their attempt to reduce immense and profound conflicts of forces, many of them lying deep in human nature, to simple moral terms. It is almost like trying to reduce a hurricane to moral terms. Unhappily, it is only when that transformation is undertaken that the interest of the American people can be aroused, or their support assured. They find it extremely difficult to grasp the concept of causation devoid of volition. They have ceased, to be sure, to see the Devil in a whirlwind, but they still see villains in all the manifestations of human biology.

One is reminded here of the Romans who mistook the rise of Christianity for a mere public disorder, to be put down by the militia.

76

THE HOPE of abolishing war is largely based upon the fact that men have long since abandoned the appeal to arms in their private disputes and submitted themselves to the jurisdiction of courts. Starting from this fact, it is contended that disputes between nations should be settled in the same manner, and that the adoption of the reform would greatly promote the happiness of the world.

Unluckily, there are three flaws in the argument. The first, which is obvious, lies in the circumstance that a system of legal remedies is of no value if it is not backed by sufficient force to impose its decisions upon even the most powerful litigants—a sheer impossibility in international affairs, for even if one powerful litigant might be coerced, it would be plainly impossible to coerce a combination, and it is precisely a combination of the powerful that is most to be feared. The second lies in the fact that any legal system, to be worthy of credit, must be administered by judges who have no personal interest in the litigation before them—another impossibility, for all the judges in the international court, in the case of disputes between first-class powers, would either be appointees of those powers, or appointees of inferior powers that were under their direct influence, or obliged to consider the effects of their enmity. The third objection lies in the fact, frequently forgotten, that the courts of justice which now exist do not actually dispense justice, but only law, and that this law is frequently in direct conflict, not only with what one litigant honestly believes to be his rights, but also with what he believes to be his honor. Practically every litigation, in truth, ends with either one litigant or the other nursing what appears to him as an outrage upon him. For both litigants to go away satisfied that justice has been done is almost unheard of.

In disputes between man and man this dissatisfaction is not of serious consequence. The aggrieved party has no feasible remedy; if he doesn't like it, he must lump it. In particular, he has no feasible remedy against a judge or a juryman who, in his view, has treated him ill; if he essayed vengeance, the whole strength of the unbiased masses of men would be exerted to destroy him, and that strength is so enormous, compared to his own puny might, that it would swiftly and certainly overwhelm him. But in the case of first-class nations there would be no such overwhelming force in restraint. In a few cases the general opinion of the world might be so largely against them that it would force them to acquiesce in the judgment rendered, but in perhaps a majority of important cases there would be sharply divided sympathies, and it would constantly encourage resistance. Against that resistance there would be nothing save the counter-resistance of the opposition—i.e., the judge against the aggrieved litigant, the twelve jurymen against the aggrieved litigant's friends, with no vast and impersonal force of neutral public opinion behind the former.

77

IT SEEMS to be generally assumed that there can be no such thing as an ugly work of art. Indeed, art and beauty are taken to be synonymous. They are, of course, nothing of the sort. A work of really appalling ugliness may show artistic skill of the first order. This was proved by the Picasso exhibition which toured the country in 1940: I saw it in Chicago. Some of the pictures displayed were extraordinarily hideous, but it was impossible to look at even the worst of them without seeing that Picasso was a highly competent painter, as indeed some of the others in the same exhibition proved abundantly. There is, in fact, no necessary connection between good painting and beauty, though the two are often found together, for most artists try to depict what they conceive to be the beautiful. But some of them have errant and absurd notions of it, and others appear to be quite indifferent to it. Even in music some indubitably adept composers appear to be incapable of it.

78

THE FACT that I have no remedy for all the sorrows of the world is no reason for my accepting yours. It simply supports the strong probability that yours is a fake.

79

IT IS impossible to imagine the universe run by a wise, just and omnipotent God, but it is quite easy to imagine it run by a board of gods. If such a board actually exists it operates precisely like the board of a corporation that is losing money.

8 0

THE FACT that the artists of a country are usually against its prevailing culture is probably a function of the fact that they are often of minority stocks. Such outlanders see it more clearly and describe it more accurately than the natives of older stock. Hence, the art of a country is predominantly critical of it. It may be, indeed, that the artistic impulse is simply a kind of disgust with things as they are. The artist is one who tries to create a better world than the one in front of him. George Santayana, despite his mysticism, described America vastly more realistically than Van Wyck Brooks. Even George Sylvester Viereck told the truth about it more often than Woodrow Wilson.

· 8 1

THE WORLD has begun to realize the dangers of universal suffrage, and in Russia and the totalitarian countries efforts have been made to get rid of them by reducing the right to vote to a mockery. But that is a poor and dishonest way to deal with the problem. It would be much more frank and rational to recognize the fact that universal suffrage will never work, and to take steps to convert the right to vote into an admitted privilege, which it obviously is. If men had to earn it by some reasonably useful service to society, it would be much greater esteemed than it is now, and exercising it in a reckless or selfish way would become more or less shameful. Today the buying of votes is countenanced by the highest authorities. The New Dealers openly advised the people on the dole to vote for its continuance.

8 2

THE IDEA of progress is intensely obnoxious to many men, and some of them devote themselves to arguing laboriously that it is an illusion. Of such sort are the learned fellows who try to prove that the ancient Greeks were more civilized than the modern Europeans. Another faction is committed to the doctrine that the scholastic philosophy of the Middle Ages was enormously superior to the common sense on which all of the sciences are based. Both of these enterprises are in vain, but nevertheless they go on.

Progress is a battle that enlists relatively few men, and on the whole they are unpopular and even disreputable. The names of Darwin and Huxley, for example, are certainly not held in honor by the generality of Americans: in Tennessee they are actually used to scare babies. This is because they devoted themselves mainly to demonstrating the falsity of ideas held to be axiomatic for long ages, but still held to be axiomatic by multitudes of simpletons. Human beings never welcome the news that something they have long cherished is untrue: they almost always reply to that news by reviling its promulgator. Nevertheless, a minority of bold and energetic men keep plugging away, and as a result of their hard labors and resultant infamy the sum of human knowledge gradually increases. Even the stupidest man of today rejects as absurd ideas that were entertained seriously by Socrates, and even the most pious nun of today hardly believes some of the nonsense that was preached by high ecclesiastical dignitaries in the Thirteenth Century. The common man contributes nothing to progress, but he nevertheless profits by it, and not only materially. His thinking is cleaner and more accurate, at least to some slight extent, than the thinking of his forebears. He may not know much that is of positive value, but he has at least got rid of many imbecilities that once flourished. To be sure, an immense number still remain, but that is simply saying that progress is a continuous process, with a future as well as a past. It is perfectly conceivable that in four or five centuries even colored clergymen may abandon their present belief in the magical potency of rabbit feet and black cats.

8 3

MAN IS one of the toughest of animated creatures. Only the anthrax bacillus can stand so unfavorable an environment for so long a time. All other mammals would succumb quickly to what man endures almost without damage. Consider, for example, the life of a soldier in the front line— or the life of anyone in Mississippi.

8 4

IN THE long run, perhaps, we'll reach a point in human progress where denying the truth will be a crime, and not only a crime but a dishonorable act. This point has been envisioned by the man who argued in *Harper's* some time ago that there is a moral obligation to be intelligent. Unless we reach it it will be vain to talk too much of human dignity, for no man can be dignified who believes anything that is palpably not true. He can be pathetic but not dignified. One may sympathize with him as one sympathizes with a child that has skinned its shin, but it is hard to convince one's self that he is really worth hell room.

All of us, to be sure, cherish delusions, but it is at least possible for a rational man to avoid the more gross and obvious ones. No one blames a man for believing that his wife is beautiful, but it is impossible to avoid disgust in the presence of one who believes that he has an immortal soul of some vaguely gaseous nature, and that it will continue to exist four hundred million years after he has been shoveled away. Such ideas are not only obviously erroneous; they are in a very true sense offensive. It is not possible to hear them stated without a kind of revulsion. The fact that they are cherished by multitudes of human beings, many of them of high virtue and not a few of them of ponderable intelligence in other respects—this fact simply proves that most of the progress of mankind still lies ahead. After all, the art of thinking must be a relatively recent acquirement. Certainly it was not possessed by Neanderthal man, at least in our sense. Neanderthal man undoubtedly had a brain, but its operations were comparable to those of a smart dog's rather than to those of an intelligent man's. It was not until skepticism arose in the world that genuine intelligence dawned. When that happened no one knows, but it was probably not more than ten thousand years ago.

8 5

THE MOST cursory glance at any Catholic treatise on moral theology is enough to show that celibate priests have a grotesquely exaggerated and inaccurate view of the relations of the sexes. That view, in many cases, is identical with the view of an adolescent. It magnifies enormously the influence of sexual impulses upon the practical business of life. They are, in fact, of relatively feeble potency, and in nine situations out of ten, and perhaps even in ninety-nine out of a hundred, they are of no potency at all. Nor is yielding to them when they emerge the calamitous matter that persons sworn to celibacy naturally assume. This yielding actually has but little durable effect on normal men and women. They soon find by experience that the ecstasy of sex, like any other powerful emotion, is self-limiting, and that after it has passed off they are substantially unchanged. It is only when sexual impulses are dammed up by conventions of one sort or another that they exert any really powerful influence upon ordinary human conduct, and even then they are a great deal less influential than, say, hunger. Very few normal persons ever do anything for purely sexual reasons, though they no doubt often believe in innocence, misled by the prevailing delusions, that they do. If all of the human beings on earth were of one sex the work of mankind would go on substantially as it does now. Life, of course, would be vastly less pleasant, but all its fundamental impetuses would remain. Women would still adorn themselves, and men would still bully and boast. There would be smart fellows getting on and poor fish complaining.

The sexual ferment at adolescence is plainly due to conventional inhibitions quite as much as to natural impulses, and that is also true of the unhealthy sexual obsession of celibates. Havelock Ellis once made the suggestion that an easy way to get rid of it would be to let adolescents experiment at will, and so reduce themselves to normalcy. This suggestion was far too sensible to be taken seriously, though it had the support of the practise of many savage tribes, who permit their children to disport freely, and believe it is beneficial. A boy or girl arriving at maturity with no sexual experience behind him or her is still an adolescent, psychologically speaking, and the adolescence thus carried into adult years may be very persistent. It forms a poor foundation for normal sexual life, and is probably the cause of many familiar catastrophes. All that stands in the way of the Ellis proposal, in Christendom, is a convention, and that convention is at least four-fifths theological. Every one of the Christian sects, however they may differ otherwise, starts out with the assumption that any act of sex is sinful, and most of them teach that it remains somewhat discreditable even after it becomes lawful. Whether or not this is true is a question that should be settled by taking objective evidence and hearing rational argument, but as things stand the discussion of it is always hushed down by loud declarations of arbitrary dogma. It is held to be wicked, not only to deny it, but even to debate it. This is the antithesis of common sense. Whenever an attempt is made to solve any human problem by such a method the result is only sound and fury.

8 6

THE THEORY that the clergy belong to the class of educated men, once well supported in fact, has persisted into our own time, though it has not been true for nearly a century. Even Protestants are commonly willing to admit that Catholic priests are what they call highly educated men. They are, of course, nothing of the sort. Nine-tenths of the knowledge that they are stuffed with is bogus, and they have very little grounding in what is really true. Since "The Origin of Species," indeed, clergymen have constituted a special class of *un*educated persons, Catholic and Protestant alike. If they happen to be naturally smart fellows they may pick up a good deal of worldly wisdom, but even that is not common. The average clergyman is a kind of intellectual eunuch comparable to a pedagogue, a Rotarian or an editorial writer.

8 7

THE IDEA that leisure is of value in itself is only conditionally true. It may be true in the case of the man who carries enough energy into his leisure to engage in some useful recreative activity, and who has intelligence enough to contribute something valuable to it. But the average man simply spends his leisure as a dog spends it. His recreations are all puerile, and the time supposed to benefit him really only stupefies him. There is some ground for believing, indeed, that leisure is dangerous. The happiest man has none. There is nothing worse than an idle hour, with no occupation offering. People who have many such hours are simply animals waiting docilely for death. We all come to that state soon or late. It is the curse of senility.

8 8

SKEPTICISM offers man the soundest of working philosophies, but it certainly does not make for happiness. The happiness of any given skeptic is always to be found, not in his doubts, but in his surviving delusions. Every member of the order has a plentiful stock of them, though he may not know it and invariably denies it. If he cherishes no other, he at least cherishes the delusion that there is one woman on earth who is an exception to all his doubts and dubieties about women in general. He may not go so far as to say he has encountered her, but he nevertheless believes that she exists, or, at worst, that she can be imagined.

8 9

THE EFFECT of every sort of New Deal is to increase and prosper the criminal class. It teaches precisely what all professional criminals believe, to wit, that it is neither virtuous nor necessary to suffer and to do without. All the old American virtues thus become ignominious, and if the thing goes on Benjamin Franklin will turn into a comic and even a sinister character. The criminal believes, like the demagogue's client, that the world owes him a living, and that it is not immoral for a have-not to seize the property of a have. Neither the criminal nor the demagogue makes any distinction between haves who acquired their property honestly and those who obtained it by chance or fraud. It is sufficient that they have it and can be made to disgorge it.

9 0

ALL GOOD literature runs against the political delusions prevailing in its time. The authors who succumbed to the war fever in 1914 all blew up before the war was over. The most tragic example was Kipling. So long as his bellowing for imperialism was only poetry it seemed charming, for no rational man expects poetry to be true, but when it appeared

that he was really serious, even his old customers began to
revolt, and he emerged from the war in ruins. In the United
States the same thing happened to many lesser fellows, for
example, Irvin Cobb. Cobb was on his way to becoming a
national figure in 1916; indeed, it was not uncommon in
those days to speak of him as the heir of Mark Twain. But
when he took to beating the drums for the Wilson balderdash he deteriorated rapidly, and by the end of the war he
was extinct.

91

THE RELATIVITY of moral ideas is proved anew every time
there is a war. Whatever the enemy does, however gallant
or reasonable, is denounced as immoral, and what the home
boys do, however brutal and dishonorable, is praised as
heroic. The gentlefolk of Virginia, perhaps the most genuinely civilized Americans ever heard of, owned slaves to
within the day of men still living, and fought a long and
bloody war in defense of the practise. By that time it was
at least as obnoxious to the rest of Christendom as, say, em-
bezzlement or adultery, yet the Virginians defended it by
arguments based upon Holy Writ, and were sufficiently convinced of its virtue to risk their lives and property for it.

92

JOHN MILTON, in his famous "Tractate of Education," laid
stress upon the need to purge the young of infantile and
adolescent concerns and concentrate their attention upon
the ideas and interests of maturity. Any adequate education, he argued, must so influence them that "they may dis-

pose and scorn all their childish and ill-taught qualities to deal with manly and liberal exercises." It must be manifest that the over-accentuation of athletics in American colleges works powerfully against this transformation. It is impossible to think of games among young men and women save as reversions to an earlier stage of growth. A really intelligent educational policy would try to discourage the taste for them, just as it tries to discourage the taste for making mud-pies.

9 3

I WAS once told by a Catholic bishop that whenever a priest comes to his ordinary with the news that he has begun to develop doubts about this or that point of doctrine, the ordinary always assumes as a matter of fact that a woman is involved. It is almost unheard of, however, for a priest to admit candidly that he is a party to a love affair: he always tries to conceal it by ascribing his desertion to theological reasons. The bishop said that the common method of dealing with such situations is to find out who the lady is, and then transfer the priest to some remote place, well out of her reach. If, after a year or two there, he still harbors his doctrinal doubts, he is permitted to withdraw quietly from his sacerdotal office and to marry her in a respectable manner, though without the blessing of the church.

9 4

MUCH more than half of the matter the American newspapers print every day is interesting only to relatively small minorities, and it is thus no wonder that the average reader reads only a small part, and falls into the mental habit of taking that small part lightly. The more reflective reader goes further: he reads next to nothing, and believes the same amount precisely. Why should he read or believe more? Every time he alights upon anything that impinges upon his own field of knowledge he discovers at once that it is inaccurate and puerile. The essential difficulty here is that journalism, to be intellecfually respectable, requires a kind of equipment in its practitioner that is necessarily rare in the world, and especially rare in a country given over to the superficial. He should have the widest conceivable range of knowledge, and he should be the sort of man who is not easily deluded by the specious and the fraudulent. Obviously, there are not enough such men to go round. The best newspaper, if it is lucky, may be able to muster half a dozen at a given moment, but the average newspaper seldom has even one. Thus American journalism (like the journalism of any other country) is predominantly paltry and worthless. Its pretensions are enormous, but its achievements are insignificant.

Even at its fundamental business of ascertaining and reporting what has happened in the world it fails miserably. Four-fifths of the so-called news it prints is dubious, and a very large proportion is downright false. Whenever a fraud with something to sell is afoot, whether in war or in peace, the great majority of journalists succumb to his blather very easily, for second- and third-rate men are always willing to follow anyone who has a loud voice, a cocksure manner, and a resilient conscience. It is a fact historians should note that, from the first outcries of the New Deal, at least four-fifths of the working journalists of the United States were for it. Opposition to it, within the ranks, was confined to a small sect of ancient cynics, who would have been equally doubtful about the Sermon on the Mount or the cellular pathology, supposing either of them new, and to newspaper proprietors, whose eyes were on their taxbills and payrolls, not upon the canons of logic, and who were and are regarded by virtually all working journalists as rogues and scoundrels.

95

IF THE proof of the merit of a government lies in its durability, then the absolutism of the Chinese takes the palm, for it lasted with little change for two thousand years. Even when it was overthrown at last all its special characters reappeared in the government that followed it—for example, its essentially aristocratic character, its arbitrary legal system, its gross corruption. There is little evidence that the Chinese proletariat has ever objected to it seriously. All the revolutions that it ever had to face, including the last one, were engineered by small minorities of ambitious men, thirsting for the spoils of power. The only difference that the fall of the Manchu monarchy made to the plain people was that they got less to eat than before, and more of them were killed.

96

THERE is no man so repulsive that he can't find a wife. Midgets, cripples, dirty men, hideous men, idiots—they are all dragged to the altar. It may be, as has been argued more than once, that women are lacking in aesthetic sensitiveness, but it is much more likely that the advantages of having a husband, especially on the lower levels, are so great that they outweigh every other consideration. The thing, of course, also runs the other way, but not to the same extent. Many a man, rolling over in bed in the morning, must be gagged by his wife, but ten times as many women have excuses for gagging. Or is this only a masculine impression, bred of the fact that a man is always more conscious of the deficiencies of other men than a woman can be expected to be, and less conscious of those of women?

97

WHEN newspapers became solvent they lost a good deal of their old venality, but at the same time they became increasingly cautious, for capital is always timid.

98

MEN ARE the only animals who devote themselves assiduously to making one another unhappy. It is, I suppose, one of their godlike qualities. Jahweh, as the Old Testament shows, spends a large part of His time trying to ruin the business and comfort of all other gods.

99

THE ENGLISH look upon all things American with contempt and dislike. That is true of absolutely all Englishmen. I have known a great many in my time, but I can't recall an exception. There are Englishmen, of course, who pretend to friendliness for the United States, but it always turns out on brief investigation that they are trying to sell something.

No Englishman really wishes this country well. He realizes only too clearly that as it rises in the world England must fall. He thus hates it as he hates Germany and Japan, and for the same reason. In addition, he adds contempt, for he is not unaware that Americans seek his good opinion and are upset when it is withheld.

This contempt is fully justified, for it is an actual fact, and can't be denied, that the United States as a nation is inferior to England. It will remain so as long as Americans, taking one with another, are susceptible to English opinion. The only cure for contempt is countercontempt. Americans will be liberated from English leading strings only when England comes to grief in the grand manner. They have survived the discovery that the English are deadbeats, and they have even learned to tolerate the idea that England seldom does its own fighting, but always hunts for mercenaries. It is not likely, however, that they would survive the discovery that England is actually incompetent, *i.e.*, inferior. Even the campaigns to put the United States into the two World Wars on the English side were grounded on the theory, diligently propagated by American Anglomaniacs, that England was still strong and that we were dependent on her defense for our own survival. That, of course, was nonsense, but the majority of Americans did not penetrate it. If they ever do so there will be a change in their attitude toward England.

100

ONE OF the reasons women crave marriage more than men is the fact that many more of them, even in these loose days, are without sexual experience. They expect something cata-

clysmic, and find only a banality that, at best, is charming, and at worst a bore. In taking to connubial bliss the
ruined girl is usually a good deal more prudent than the
virgin.

101

ONE OF the chief functions of religion is that of time-bind-
ing. It determines values and then fixes them. Thus Christianity has preserved the ethics of the Jews for nearly two
thousand years. They are valid today only in exceptional circumstances, and yet all Christians at least give them lip service. Man always fears change. More of his institutions—
for example, government and marriage—are devices to prevent it, or, at all events, to delay it. An ordinary corporation
is another such device. Who would rebel if the fruits of re-
bellions were thought of as only transient? Every rebel believes that he is bringing in a new day that will last. The
new values that he invents assume in his mind the status
of permanent and immutable values, and he resents bitterly
any suggestion of change in them, however trivial. Jefferson
would have killed himself if he could have seen ahead to
Roosevelt II.

Man tries to protect himself against change even beyond the grave: he acquires property; he generates children.
Moved by the yearning for fame, he spends immense energy
on work that cannot conceivably get him any reward until
after he is dead. He has never accepted the plain biological
fact that all his moods, experiences and needs are essentially
transient. He is always trying to freeze them. He hates
change in them more than he hates anything else in the
cosmos.

102

ANY SEX relation is bound to be full of peril, if only because it is a situation in which people lose their heads and act on instinct. Every such situation is full of hazards, no matter how much poetry may embellish it or logic justify it.

103

THE FEMALE moron, in her capacity as parasite, is frequently able to conceal her low intelligence, for the world is very apt to judge women by their clothes. Thus the stupidity of those on the lower intellectual levels may be concealed as effectively as the intelligence of those on the higher. A woman of real brilliance is often disdainful of the conventions which oppress her sex, including especially the conventions of fashion, and so appears before the world as a dowdy. The female moron, on the contrary, employs every device that is calculated to arrest the attention of unobservant men, and in consequence she often marries well. Not uncommonly her imbecility is revealed dramatically when her first husband dies, for with money in her purse she usually tracks down a second who would disgrace a ten-cent-store girl. Many such well-heeled but hollow-headed widows marry movie actors, and there was once a Vanderbilt relict who made off with a prize-fighter. Here it is not to be forgotten that the possession of wealth, or of a glib tongue, or of some other such factitious aid is of great value also to males of low mental visibility. Many of them rise to high places in commerce and industry, and some have got on so well in politics that they have become serious contenders for the Presidency.

104

THERE is an invariable tendency among inferior men to magnify their own importance and puissance by organizing a party. This tendency is clearly visible in the literary field. The so-called Regionalists of the South, who made a great pother in the 1930 era, were simply a gang of eighth-rate poets who fought to give their maundering some dignity by ascribing to it a profound political purpose. The same thing was true of the Imagists, and of the so-called proletarians. My hardest job in the days when I was writing book reviews was to break up the Mencken party. It was constantly forming itself, and constantly disgracing me. My belief is that such parties never accomplish anything valuable. They fall inevitably into the hands of crooked and self-seeking men, and in a little while they are full of obviously dubious doctrines. All of them attempt to discipline their members. The Regionalists were always quarreling among themselves, just as the Humanists of Irving Babbitt used to quarrel. The proletarians went so far as to hold heresy trials. The literature of the world is not written by such joiners. It is the exclusive product of independent men. One of their chief marks, indeed, is the fact that they do *not* believe what is generally believed, even by men of their trade.

105

No MATTER how drastically successive waves of labor legislation cut down working-hours, it will still remain true that, in the long run, the diligent and competent get on best.

106

SUICIDE is commonly frowned upon, and by English law it still remains a felony. This disfavor, which originated in theological concepts, is hard to justify on social grounds. I have known a good many men and women who took their own lives, but I can't think of one whose decision was illogical. Nine times out of ten they sought escape from truly unendurable situations and ten times out of ten they pronounced admirable self-judgments. It would be difficult, and perhaps downright impossible, to justify rationally the continued survival of anyone convinced that he should end his life.

107

CAN THE United States ever become genuinely civilized? Certainly it is possible. Even Scotland has made enormous progress since the Eighteenth Century, when, according to Macaulay, most of it was on the cultural level of Albania. The Japanese, in less than a century, have climbed into the first rank of World Powers, and their advance has been as great in the useful sciences as in war and commerce. Even Mississippi, on some remote tomorrow, may reach the estate of Poland between the two World Wars.

108

THE FREEDOM of nations is of little human value. It is only the liberty of the individual that counts. Imperialistic conquest often actually widens it. This is obviously the case in India. In the days of native rule no citizen had any rights whatsoever. Under the English he has a long series of them, and some of them are more or less real and valuable.

109

THE BOORISHNESS cultivated by Communists is analogous to going into company without a necktie. Certain Communists actually affect the latter. Even George Bernard Shaw insisted on wearing clothes that were grotesque and conspicuous. No decently bred man ever does anything of the sort.

110

THE MORE vocal and ambitious American Negroes talk constantly of their desire for all the common rights of the American Caucasian, but what they really have in mind, in most cases, is his privileges—for example, his privilege of going at will into any society or environment that attracts him. It must be manifest that such privileges will never be granted to any minority that is sharply differentiated. They are, in fact, denied to large numbers of whites. The Negroes are quite right in alleging that, in their own case, these denials are commonly based upon their color alone, and not on any objective proof of inferiority or experience of ill behavior. What they forget is that color is the most crass and inescapable of all differentiations. The Caucasian is aware of it the moment one of them appears, and whether consciously or unconsciously it annoys him as an invasion of his natural human preference for his own kind.

The fact that what are commonly spoken of as rights are often really privileges is demonstrated in the case of the Jews. They resent bitterly their exclusion from certain hotels, resorts and other places of gathering, and make determined efforts to horn in. But the moment any considerable number of them horns in the attractions of the place diminish, and the more pushful Jews turn to one where they are still *nicht gewünscht*. The discontented Negro often shows something of the same irrationality, though not often in so bellicose a manner. My guess is that if they were suddenly admitted to the hotels that now bar them the first comers would quickly support the exclusion of the rest. A Negro enjoys lording it over other Negroes almost as much as a white cracker of Georgia enjoys it.

I I I

WE HAVE long been taught that democracy and liberty are indistinguishable, but experience proves that this is not true. The two have been confused by the jabbering of mountebanks. They are, in most situations, in direct opposition. The true democrat is a kind of religious fanatic. He simply can't imagine another man doubting democracy. Any such doubt is a heresy, and by his theory, an extremely dangerous heresy. Hence, he is always trying to put it down. There was more free speech in the Prussia of Frederick the Great, the last Asiatic despot of Western Europe, than there has ever been in any democratic state. To be sure, a certain amount of liberty is usually on tap in the democracies, but it is only as a sort of luxury for hours of ease. Whenever the state is menaced its first measure is to try to put all liberty down.

112

Uplifters of all sorts spend their time cadging money from A to save the so-called underprivileged B. Once they settle down to their business the cadging of this money becomes an end in itself, and they'd keep on doing it even if all the underprivileged were succored. Even setting aside considerations of their private profit, it must be manifest that they are moved largely by mere professional zeal. Every quack always ends by convincing himself that his quackery is a boon to humanity. It is impossible to convince any given uplifter that the world would still go on if his graft were abolished.

113

What men consider to be sound and desirable determines the whole course of their thinking. The Egyptians, by laying a foolish stress on the preservation of the body postmortem, wrecked their whole intellectual system. Egypt became a country, not of ideas, but of memories.

114

The man who accumulates any considerable property discovers for himself that the mere accumulation of it is no fun. He thereupon turns to other enterprises, and the result is that four out of five rich men become uplifters of one sort or another. The only man who is really dominated by the profit motive is the small fellow. Many a village mortgage shark yields to it completely, but I have never encountered a rich city man who did not ameliorate it with some other form of yearning. Even Russell Sage in his old age took to philanthropy. Such a person as Hetty Green is a pathological case, and so rare as to be a kind of curiosity.

115

THE CURRENT sentimentalizing of the old-time family doctor is, like any other sentimentality, mainly buncombe. In ninety-nine medical situations out of a hundred it is of no advantage to a doctor to know his patient intimately. On the contrary, it is often a disadvantage. To be sure, it is pleasant to the patient to be on agreeable terms with his doctor, but it is certainly not necessary to be an intimate friend. A good doctor can find out all that he needs to know without drawing on a lifetime of private acquaintance—indeed, it is probably safer to patronize doctors who are not actual friends, for they are more objective in their approach, and it is the shrewdly objective approach that counts in medicine, and especially in diagnosis. The idea that a doctor should be a family friend flows out of the prevailing delusion that most illnesses are largely psychic. This nonsense has been preached so long that many otherwise intelligent people, including even doctors, believe it. It is very seldom true. The influence of the mind on the body is ponderable, but it is infinitely less than the influence of the body on the mind. The cart here is often put before the horse; in fact, it is habitually put before the horse.

The best doctor is not one who has had years of experience with the actual patient before him, but one who has had years of experience with multitudes of other patients. That is why the specialist is more effective than the general practitioner. He is simply a man who has seen the situation now confronting him a great many times, and is familiar with its variations. The general practitioner at best can have seen it only a few times, and his memories of it are blurred by a crowd of memories of other situations, some of them deceptively like it.

The best the family doctor can do, facing situations of any seriousness, is to sort out patients for specialists. Even in the most trivial diseases his skill is bound to be very limited. Private medicine should be reorganized on the plan set up in the dispensaries of good hospitals. In such places a single medical man of proved shrewdness sees the patients as they come in. He makes snap diagnoses, and sends them to this or that special clinic. Now and then he falls into error, but it is hardly important, for the specialists quickly recognize it and rectify it. Nine times out of ten his guess turns out to be more or less correct. After all, there is nothing particularly esoteric about the symptoms of the more common diseases. It may happen now and then that even a good medical man mistakes a case of pneumonia for a broken leg, but it is certainly not frequent.

The chief area of errors is the abdominal region, where symptoms are often obscure and those of quite different diseases are deceptively similar. But in this region as in others, the specialist has enormous advantages over the family doctor—indeed, his advantages are so gigantic that the family doctor's work could be dismissed as trivial if doing it badly were not so dangerous. All the errors that lead to burst appendixes are made by family doctors. The patient is usually sick enough to call for help, but by the time he gets to the specialist he is too far gone for it. Such errors are always made by family doctors who are supposed to know the patient inside and out. While they gossip with him, with occasional glances at his tongue, and inquire about his mother-in-law's asthma, his burst appendix is pouring pathogenic organisms into his abdominal cavity.

The ideal medical system would have a first line of diagnosticians at least as good as the young residents who function in the dispensaries of first-rate hospitals, and behind that line it would set up a rank of really competent specialists, including specialists in such commonplace trivialities as colds in the head. Very few colds in the head, in fact, are simply colds in the head. It is highly probable that an actually healthy individual would never have them. Unfortunately, few such individuals are known. The human body is a complex organism in a state of dubious equilibrium. It is almost unthinkable for all parts of it to be operating perfectly at any one time. It may happen now and then, but certainly it is not frequent. Investigation would probably show that it is so rare as to be a kind of disease. I have never known any really observant person who wasn't more or less uncomfortable all the time.

116

THE TRUE history of World War II, like that of World War I, will probably never be written. The professional historians, as usual, will swallow the official doctrine, which is palpably false. They will take every scrap of official document seriously, and even accept with gravity the reports of the newspapers. It is not hard for a man of reasonable intelligence to get some glimpses of the process by which the United States was hauled into the war, but there are great gaps in the record, and it is not to the interest of anyone concerned to fill them. All that can be established with fair certainty is that no account of the matter by Roosevelt II and his followers will be even so much as half true. Their version, whatever it is, will conceal many essential facts, and apply a heavy coating of cosmetics to motives. Maybe some measure of the truth will be unearthed in the years to come, but probably not. Despite all the excavations that have been undertaken, the history of the American Revolution remains more or less mysterious—and largely incredible. The manufacturers of school histories, of course, will accept the official doctrine about World War II without a thought of challenging it, and in consequence the Americans of the future will know no more about it than they know about World War I, or the Spanish-American War, or indeed the Civil War. In the whole body of "facts" that they are taught to believe, no more than 10 per cent. will be true. The rest will be evasion, sentimentalization, downright lying.

117

THE MARYLAND Legislature, I suppose, is typical of all American State Legislatures. It is neither worse than the average nor better than the average, and it thus supports Maryland's tendency to occupy a middle place in all American tables of statistics. The population of the State is almost evenly balanced between the inhabitants of Baltimore and those of the counties, but, as usual, the counties have proportionately more votes. Nevertheless, the late Albert C. Ritchie, while he was Governor of Maryland, told me that the county members, on the whole, were better than the city members. A certain honor still attached to membership in the rural regions, especially to membership in the State Senate, for a senator retains his title for life, by custom if not by law. But the city members tend more and more to be mere ward-heelers, nominated and elected by professional politicians. Now and then a capable and honest man appears among them, but it is very unusual. As a result, the Legislature is extremely backward, intellectually speaking, and seldom originates a really sound piece of legislation. All such improvements and reforms are forced upon it from without, often with great difficulty. The one apparent aim of nine members out of ten is to grab as much money as they can get for their bailiwicks and as many jobs as possible for their supporters. It is almost unheard of for one of them to show any rational interest in the welfare of the State as a whole.

118

THERE is no possibility whatsoever of reconciling science and theology, at least in Christendom. Either Jesus arose from the dead or He didn't. If He did, then Christianity becomes plausible; if He did not, then it is sheer nonsense. I defy any genuine scientist to say that he believes in the Resurrection, or indeed in any other cardinal dogma of the Christian system. They are all grounded upon statements of fact that are intrinsically incredible. Those so-called scientists who profess to accept them are not scientists at all—for example, the late Howard A. Kelly. Kelly was simply an extraordinarily skillful and successful virtuoso of technic, comparable to a champion golfer or buck-and-wing dancer. He made a few more or less useful contributions to surgical mechanics, but so far as I know he has made none whatever to the science of medicine. Nicholas W. Alter, who used to be his pathologist, once told me that he was a complete dud at the microscope. Alter swore, in fact, that Kelly couldn't distinguish between a section of sarcoma and a slice of beefsteak.

The current revolt against the so-called liberal theology is perfectly sound. That theology is nothing save an excuse and an evasion. It reduces both science and theology to the ridiculous. If a man can't believe that Jesus arose from the dead he should say so frankly and have done. It is not only foolish but also dishonest for him to pretend to accept all the implications of Christianity without admitting the basic postulate. In this field the Catholic Church, as usual, has been enormously more intelligent than the Protestant. It has rejected so-called Modernism in toto and refuses any compromise with it. The Protestants' attempts to compromise have simply made Protestantism ludicrous. No man of any intellectual dignity can accept it, or even discuss it seriously. The only really respectable Protestants are the Fundamentalists. Unfortunately, they are also palpable idiots, and so Christianity gains nothing by their adherence —in fact, it is gravely injured by their adherence, just as spiritualism would be made preposterous, even if it were not so intrinsically, by the frowsy old imbeciles who believe in it.

119

ALL THE great enterprises of the world are run by a few smart men: their aids and associates run down by rapid stages to the level of sheer morons. Everyone knows that this is true of government, but we often forget that it is equally true of private undertakings. In the average great bank, or railroad, or other corporation the burden of management lies upon a small group. The rest are ciphers.

120

THE IDEA of restitution seems to have disappeared from our criminal law—a sad loss indeed. Why shouldn't the criminal who has inflicted wanton loss or damage on a decent citizen be forced to make it good? It should be easily possible to require him to do so. Let him be put to work on public work, and all his earnings above the cost of his subsistence and policing handed over to his victim. That victim seems to be forgotten today. We are taught that the punishment of the criminal, whatever it may be, is not *his* revenge, but society's. Yet to society it involves a continuing expense, and the victim gets nothing—not even the costs of prosecution. Sometimes those costs are formidable. Not infrequently, indeed, they dissuade him from proceeding, and the criminal escapes.

At the time the late Judge Joseph N. Ulman of Baltimore (1878–1943) was chairman of a committee appointed to investigate prison labor I suggested to him that the idea of restitution be revived. He professed interest in it, but nothing was done. The majority of so-called penologists, I gather, are against it, as they are against every other scheme to introduce rationality into the criminal law. Certainly the man who has been robbed should get his money back, and equally certainly the man who has been injured should be indemnified for all his expenses, with punitive damages added for his sufferings. As things stand, a solvent criminal may be sued civilly but there are so few solvent criminals that this remedy is worth nothing. I have never, in fact, heard of it being resorted to.

In case of murder I think it should be written into the law that no murderer, under any circumstances whatever, shall ever be released until his victim's natural expectation of life has expired. There is no reason that I can imagine why he should enjoy liberty while that victim is deprived of life.

121

THE CONCEPT of impersonal natural law is hard to grasp, and all save a small minority of men seem to be unable to do so. They see human volition, and usually human malice, in every event, especially on the economic level, just as a savage sees a human-like volition in a stroke of lightning. It is impossible for them to take in the idea that their fellow-men are often, and perhaps even usually, no more than the tools of irresistible natural forces, just as they are themselves.

122

IF THE abolition of war were really possible it would be a pity to lose an enterprise that has given so much delight to mankind. It remains the greatest of sports, and I am convinced that the overwhelming majority of those who are forced to engage in it enjoy it, and look back upon it afterward with high satisfaction. To be sure, they commonly make some effort to evade service, but once they are collared they make the best of it, and presently discover that that best is very far from unpleasant. This was certainly true of the conscripts in World War II. All save a small minority of them came from environments a great deal less comfortable than an Army camp, or even than front-line quarters, and all save the same few came from jobs (or the expectation of jobs) much less varied and amusing than that of a soldier. At one stroke they were relieved of that haunting uncertainty about subsistence which is the curse of all poor and ignorant young men, and also of all need to experiment and decide for themselves. They were fed and clothed at the public expense, the work they were called upon to do was irregular and not usually onerous, they had money to jingle in their pockets, they were taken on interesting tours of far places, and they had a great deal of personal liberty, and could engage freely in sports and other divertissements forbidden in their native places. Their lives, in brief, were not unlike those of the inmates of a well-run prison, but with no lock-up at night, no high walls, very little dull labor, and the constant expectation of release on some near tomorrow—not as wards of nosey cops and parole officers, but as heroes. The decisions that harass a simple-minded man did not bother them at all. Not only did someone else decide what they should wear, where they should sleep, when they should get up and when they should go to bed, and what they should eat and when: all these accommodations were provided for them plentifully, and at no expense to themselves. In brief, the burden of responsibility was lifted from them altogether. Nor were they concerned about the support and welfare of their dependents, if any, for such things were the care of the mysterious and god-like powers above them. Finally, they had no reason to fear that they would starve if disabled, or that their dependents would starve in case of their own deaths, for the government had undertaken to supply all necessities, and even certain luxuries, in either case.

I speak here, of course, of average soldiers—the conscripts from the farms, the poor fellows in bad jobs, the boys just out of school. There was, of course, a minority to whom conscription meant a heavy loss of something valuable, but that minority was not large. The average soldier left behind him only what the average American had had in peace time, to wit, a wearisome and badly rewarded job, with small prospect of anything better thereafter. In place of this dull drudgery he found in the Army a vastly more spacious life, with many of the privileges of a chartered libertine. If he had dreamed of travel it was a vain dream, but now he travelled on conducted tours quite as comfortable, much more entertaining and enormously less expensive than any ever arranged by Cook. If he got drunk he might be punished lightly, but his punishment never involved the loss of his job. If he engaged in fornication it was a venial sin, not reprehended by his superiors unless he picked up some venereal disease. If he did a little stealing it was one of his privileges as a savior of humanity. If he was rough and brutal it was a sign of his fighting spirit. Moreover, he could look forward to distinction and respect for the rest of his life, with a long list of special privileges. In every community in America, however small, there are local notables whose notability rests wholly on the fact that they were once drafted into some war or other. Their services were probably trivial and they took up service reluctantly, but nevertheless they are now men of mark, and insist on having a voice in all communal affairs. Their general intelligence is shown by the kind of ideas they advocate. They are, in the main, bitter enemies of the liberty of the individual, and are responsible for some of the worst corruptions of politics. The most grasping of all politicians is the war veteran.

123

THE IDEA that science is arid is due to a lack of imagination in those who propagate it. What was arid in the work of Koch? Or in that of Pasteur? Or even in that of Darwin? The same people who make this argument are usually prepared to believe that theology is a rich and charming science, or that Marx and his disciples were profound thinkers. They are the kind of men who dislike instinctively whatever is intellectually decent and probably true. Such men exist in the world in large numbers. They are as easily recognizable as the men who dislike physical cleanliness. Indeed, it is hard to find any essential difference, logically speaking, between wearing a dirty collar and believing in Calvin or Marx.

124

THE SOCIALIZED medicine scheme, even assuming it to be rational, plainly needs certain amendments. It would be brutal to inflict scientific medicine upon the generality of American morons, for they never turn to it when they have clear choice. They always prefer patent medicine, chiropractic, faith healing or something worse. If the Federal bureaucracy ever really takes over the job of looking at their tongues, it should choose as its agents, not graduates of Class A medical schools, but such Hippocrateses of the folk as the heirs and assigns of Lydia Pinkham, Dr. Munyon, Brinkley (the goat gland man), and Mary Baker G. Eddy.

125

THE BELIEVING mind is eternally impervious to evidence. The most that can be accomplished with it is to induce it to substitute one delusion for another. It rejects all overt evidence as wicked. Thus Americans in general go on whooping up democracy, though every even half intelligent American, put on the stand, will admit freely that it is full of holes. In the same way Christianity survives, though very few Christians believe in it at all, and only a small company of admittedly psychopaths believe in it altogether. Put into the form of an affidavit, what the latter profess to regard as true would make even the Pope laugh.

126

A SHOW of altruism is respected in the world chiefly for selfish motives—the usual human paradox. Everyone figures himself profiting by it tomorrow. It thus becomes creditable, and hence profitable, to the one who exhibits it. It makes him popular. In most cases that is probably all there is in it.

127

THE PUBLIC schools of the United States were damaged very seriously when they were taken over by the State. So long as they were privately operated the persons in charge of them retained a certain amount of professional autonomy, and with it went a considerable dignity. But now they are all petty jobholders, and show the psychology that goes with the trade. They have invented a bogus science of pedagogy to salve their egos, but it remains hollow to any intelligent eye. What they may teach or not teach is not determined by themselves, or even by any exercise of sound reason, but by the interaction of politics on the one side and quack theorists on the other. Even savages have reached a better solution of the educational problem. Their boys are taught, not by puerile eunuchs, but by their best men, and the process of education among them really educates. This is certainly not true of ours. Many a boy of really fine mind is ruined in school. Along with a few sound values, many false ones are thrust into his thinking, and he inevitably acquires something of the attitude of mind of the petty bureaucrats told off to teach him. In college he may recover somewhat, for the college teacher is relatively more free than the pedagogue lower down the scale. But even in college education has become corrupted by buncombe, and so the boy on the border line of intelligence is apt to be damaged rather than benefited. Under proper care he might be pushed upward. As it is, he is shoved downward. Certainly everyday observation shows that the average college course produces no visible augmentation in the intellectual equipment and capacity of the student. Not long ago, in fact, an actual investigation in Pennsylvania demonstrated that students often regress so much during their four years that the average senior is less intelligent, by all known tests, than the average freshman. Part of this may be due to the fact that many really intelligent boys, as soon as they discover the vanity of the so-called education on tap, quit college in disgust, but in large part, I suspect, it is a product of the deadening effect of pedagogy.

128

ROSE MACAULAY shows in "Some Religious Elements in English Literature" (Harcourt, 1931) that during the Eighteenth Century very few presumably enlightened Englishmen actually threw off Christianity. On the Continent there was a marked tendency toward rationalism, and the same thing was witnessed in the American colonies. But in England, always a bit backward intellectually, there was a considerable holding back, and even such philosophers as Locke, Berkeley and Hobbes hesitated to reject the official theology altogether. Among the resigning literati only Pope showed any inclination toward what was then called Deism, and he was very careful to avoid offense. Addison, Steele, Johnson, Swift and the rest remained faithful to the state church to the end of their days.

129

LIFE has been defined as irritability, which is to say, the capacity to suffer. It is impossible to imagine a living creature that cannot be hurt. Even an amoeba quickly spits out distasteful particles, and makes tracks when he sees more coming along.

130

OF ALL the fine schemes of the so-called pacifists, perhaps the most absurd is the proposal that the question of war or peace be submitted to popular vote. If this were done the last impediment to the demagogy would be gone. Given a week of unchallenged radio crooning, and Roosevelt II could have persuaded the American plain people to the most fantastic war imaginable. The case of the national attitude toward Finland in World War II offers sufficient proof. One day the Finns were a brave people fighting for self-determination; a week later, on precisely the same evidence, they were wicked enemies of democracy.

131

ROTATION in office is probably a bad idea. We have had to ameliorate it by the Civil Service and by various other devices. The set term is a dreadful burden upon every elected official, even when he happens to be able and conscientious. A good President, like a bad President, has to begin running for re-election the day after he is inaugurated. If he could be kept in office during good behavior, like a judge, he would show the independence that many judges now show.

132

THE MOST modern poets have been the English. No other
country can match the line stretching from Wordsworth to
Kipling. By the same token England has been notably backward in all the other arts. This seems to me to be an indication that English civilization is somewhat behind the
procession, for poetry belongs to a relatively early stage of
culture.

133

THE AMERICAN, more than any other man, is prone to be
apologetic about the trade he follows. He seldom believes
that it is worthy of his dignity and talents, and in consequence he dreams almost normally of abandoning it for
something more glorious. This is true, to a surprisingly large
extent, even of men in the so-called learned professions. Most
American lawyers, for example, seem to be willing at any
time to abandon their trade for political office, or for cushy
posts with corporations. The same willingness is visible in
university professors, who began to throw off their gowns
to take secular employment in the Coolidge Golden Age,
and later flocked to the New Deal in almost countless numbers. Even American medical men, taking one with another,
seem to be dubious and apologetic about their profession,
and a formidable minority of them are apparently quite
willing to accept state medicine and so take humble places
at the public teat. Indeed, it is only a small minority, made
up almost wholly of the extraordinarily successful, who view
this prospect with genuine horror. Of the clergy I need
hardly speak. It would be hard indeed to find an American

pastor who is irrevocably unwilling to throw off his chasuble for some well-paid branch of the uplift.

On the lower levels of human endeavor, from which complete escape is commonly more difficult, the sufferers seek surcease by pretending that their trade is much loftier than it is in fact. This explains the enormous proliferation of such absurd euphemisms as *mortician* and *realtor*. They make the judicious grieve, but they offer a very real consolation and reassurance to men who sweat in vain against what they conceive to be the meanness of their trade. The same effort to escape is visible in the movement headed and symbolized by Rotary. The central purpose here is plainly to convince a miscellany of unfelonious but unhappily unimportant men that they are really citizens of mark, whose opinions upon all public matters deserve to be heard and attended to. But Rotary is snobbish in its choice of members, and so are all its imitations in their descending order, and in consequence the vast majority of Americans must remain in the outer dark, sore and unsatisfied.

The psychological effects of their discontent deserve serious investigation. It is, I believe, sufficiently established that a man in revolt against his lot always transforms his rebellion into hatred of those who, by his standards, stand above him. He begins by envying them, and he ends by trying to rob them of their advantage, usually under cover of a lofty moral purpose. This process lies at the bottom of democracy, and it is thus no wonder that the democratic dogma is most esteemed in the country in which the largest proportion of people are ashamed of their jobs.

134

MOST of the American professors educated in Germany—but certainly not all—howled against the German *Kultur* in World War I, though nearly all of them had whooped it up before the band began to play. In part they yielded to the quick and vicious attack of their colleagues who had *not* been educated in Germany. These last, for many years, had been the targets of their sneers, and naturally took advantage of the first chance to get revenge on them. In other part, the professors gave way to pressure from trustees and alumni, who were predominantly Anglophil, as all well-heeled Americans tend to be Anglophil. Finally, there was the cowardice that is one of the characteristic marks of the craft. A professor, even at his best, is a pedagogue, and a pedagogue is seldom much of a man.

135

DEMOCRACY lasted, in the United States, almost precisely 150 years. Its decline was not by catastrophe, but by a slow and stealthy reductio ad absurdum. There were times when it seemed to be reviving, but that appearance was illusory. It was a great deal nearer its death struggles in the Civil War era, when Walt Whitman wrote about it so ecstatically, than it had been in Jefferson's day. The election of Roosevelt II, in 1932, gave it the *coup de grâce*.

136

ONE OF the fellows I can't understand is the man with violent likes and dislikes in his drams—the man who dotes on highballs but can't abide malt liquor, or who drinks white wine but not red, or who holds that Scotch whiskey benefits his kidneys whereas rye whiskey corrodes his liver. As for me, I am prepared to admit some merit in every alcoholic beverage ever devised by the incomparable brain of man, and drink them all when the occasions are suitable—wine with meat, the hard liquors when my so-called soul languishes, beer to let me down gently of an evening. In other words, I am omnibibulous, or, more simply, ombibulous.

137

IN LITERATURE, as in life, it is extremely perilous to cherish false values. But cherishing them goes on, and one of its results is the common academic notion, rammed into generations of poor schoolboys, that Bunyan's "Pilgrim's Progress" belongs to the grand literature of the world. It is actually on all fours, in its ideational content, with the Book of Mormon, "Science and Health," and the Egyptian Book of the Dead. I had almost added Calvin's "Institutes" and Swedenborg's "Arcana Coelestia." As a piece of writing it is measurably better, but even here it is only a pastiche of stealings from the King James Bible, badly selected and clumsily put together.

138

THE UNRELIABILITY of history is one of the crying scandals of civilization. To this day no really convincing account of the origins of the Civil War has been written. Worse, there exists no adequate history of the United States. When historians began to turn to so-called "sources" they undoubtedly made a step toward accuracy, but it is now evident that most sources offer no more than special pleading, and hence are almost indistinguishable from what are now called press-agents' hand-outs. James Ford Rhodes apparently made a further step when he began to mine contemporary news-papers, but it is hard to believe that anyone forced to read American newspapers during World War II will ever be-lieve in them again. In all probability it will be eternally impossible to arrive at the precise truth about the majority of salient historical events. At best, only half of the story can ever be known. Worse, there is little indication that historians, as a class, have any actual desire to establish even that half. Those of the academic moiety seldom lift themselves above the level of mere pedagogues, and those outside the fold are commonly highly prejudiced partisans. It would be hard to imagine honest history being written by Woodrow Wilson on the one hand or Henry Cabot Lodge on the other, yet both have respectable places as American historians, and are in fact rather more reliable than most. The best are probably chance bystanders—for example, Gideon Welles. Welles set up his famous diary, I suspect, because he was uncomfortably aware that what was generally believed about the Civil War and its chief actors was not true. But having written it, he began to realize that the truth was not generally relished, so he kept it secret, and it was not published until 1912, a third of a century after his death.

Autobiography, though it always makes interesting reading, is hardly more to be trusted than academic history. It seems to be almost impossible for a man who has had a hand in great events to tell the truth about them. Even the narratives of such realistic and iconoclastic fellows as William T. Sherman and of such dull, unimaginative clods as U. S. Grant are full of palpable evasions. If Woodrow Wilson had written his autobiography it would have been a genuine marvel of false pretenses. Even among the official histories it would have stood out in that respect. Less puissant men sometimes make an effort to tell the truth, but save in a few exceptional cases they do not know what it is.

139

IF THEOLOGY were really one of the sciences its professors would devote themselves assiduously to what is called psychical research. They cannot object to it on the ground that it is infested by quacks, for their own art and mystery, on their own showing, is also infested by quacks; indeed, they give over a large part of their time and energy to exposing and denouncing such quacks, *i.e.*, to arguing that the pastor in the next tabernacle preaches heresy. But it is rare to find a theologian who shows any interest in the effort to prove by objective evidence that man has an immortal soul—the fundamental postulate of their whole idology. What makes them shy of it, I suspect, is a haunting fear that it will not only fail to produce proofs positive that man survives bodily death, but maybe produce proofs that he doesn't.

140

THE CHRISTIAN idea that it is a merit to do no evil, even to the evil-doer, and to make no resistance, no matter how gross the provocation—this idea, of course, is much older than Christianity. It appears in the primeval Indian cults under the name of *Ahimsa*. It has worked very badly in India, and it is working so badly in Christendom that, as a practical matter, few Christians ever give it a thought. Even the Quakers, who are specially committed to it, do not stress it in their daily life. Try to get a dollar out of one of them, and he will not only defend it stoutly; he will also try to wrest another dollar out of *you* as punitive damages.

141

CASUISTRY has got a bad name in the world, mainly, I suppose, because of the dubious uses to which it was put during the Sixteenth and Seventeenth Centuries by some of its Jesuit practitioners. But it is really a very useful art, and its influence upon the thinking of mankind has probably been much more beneficial than deleterious. Some of the most valuable liberties of the modern age were attained by the use of adept casuistry. It was impossible to argue for them openly, but they could be supported effectively by the tricks invented by theological casuists. The legal fictions that broke down the old rigidity of English law had the same origin. It is a pity that American law is not developing more of them.

142

HAS ANY child psychologist ever noted that the talk of small boys among themselves consists almost entirely of boasting? Every boy devotes himself to telling how strong his father is, or how rich or how adept at all manly sports, or how greatly the family refrigerator surpasses all other refrigerators, or how many costly and incomparable toys he got at

Christmas, or how many cats the family dog has killed, or
how many rats the family cat has killed, and so on. I often
stop to watch small boys at play, and listen to them. They
are all show-offs. I suppose that the talk of little girls runs
the same way, but I am not sure. If there is no scientific
treatise on the subject, equipped with all the usual tables
and graphs, then there surely ought to be one.

143

IN WORLD WAR I the lady soldiers of democracy wore a
garb imitating the male uniform. The result was disastrous,
for the bulges of their hips and breasts were made grotesquely conspicuous. In World War II the WAC's and
their sisters were outfitted with uniforms frankly feminine,
and competent dress designers were employed to devise
them. There was, in consequence, an enormous improvement in the appearance of the female military, and attempts
upon their virtue were much more numerous than in World
War I. In 1944 it was reported from Washington that the
WAC's official equipment had been reinforced with con-
traceptive apparatus.

144

THE BELIEF that man is immortal is a vestige of the childish
egoism which once made him believe that the earth is the
center of the solar system. This last is probably still cherished by four Americans out of five.

145

THE AVERAGE low-down man, consumed by his envy of his
betters, can see only one distinction between man and

man, and that is the distinction of _wealth_. He believes that
he would be fully the equal of his betters if he had as much
money. All other superiorities are hidden from him save
those that are even more factitious than the superiority of
wealth—for example, that of a politician, or that of a movie
actor—and even in these areas wealth is a potent factor. A
bankrupt movie actor would not be admired.

146

WHEN religion began to fade out of the colleges the teaching of ethics went with it. But the need for such teaching
still exists, and its disappearance has had many unpleasant
consequences. Not a few college students of today lack even
common politeness. They get no training in it at home, and
their teachers no longer take any active interest in their
conduct. I am speaking here, of course, of colleges really
worthy of the name. In the fifth-rate denominational schools
moral theology is still taught furiously, but inasmuch as its
professors are complete idiots, its effects are deleterious
rather than beneficial. The moral system that it inculcates
is fit only for yahoos.

147

THE NOTION that it is against human nature to want to die
is as absurd as the old notion that it is against human nature to have no yearning for immortality. Many men, in
fact, show an active desire to die and have it over. Every
suicide proves this more or less. The case of George East-
man proved it massively. William H. Welch did not commit suicide, yet he made plain efforts to shorten the agony

of his last days. He refused all treatment, and even objected to it when his attendants proposed to wash him. In the end, he simply turned his face to the wall and held his breath. His death was really a kind of suicide. He had made up his mind that he was incurable and that life was no longer worth living. He was right.

148

IT WOULD be interesting to hear argument in favor of the doctrine that it is one of the functions of government to provide a job for every citizen. That doctrine, in fact, is palpable nonsense. If it were true then the government would have to determine the occupation of every man, and the commonest of liberties would vanish. The correspondence schools advertise that they can make a Diesel engineer of anyone not downright imbecile, or a radio operator, or a postal clerk. Is the government bound to provide jobs for all their graduates, or is it free to set the nascent Diesel engineer or postal clerk to pushing a wheelbarrow? So far as I know, no advocate of the jobs-for-all balderdash has undertaken to answer this obvious and inescapable question.

149

THE MERIT of many human acts is no more than a function of their difficulty. We esteem whatever doing is hard doing, rarely done well. This may account for the superiority of honor to common morality in the eyes of those capable of it. They know that most men are not.

150

THE NEW DEALERS, ostensibly trying to put an end to unjust and irrational forays by the haves, only opened the
way for unjust and irrational forays by the have-nots. It was
quite as immoral to pay a farmer bonuses out of the taxpayers' money as it had been to pay a manufacturer bonuses
through the tariff system. By 1940 any pressure group able
to muster enough votes to scare politicians could obtain
anything it pleased, regardless alike of constitutional law
and of common justice. The Constitution was converted
into a rubber garment able to fit any situation favorable to
politicians. All its irrevocable guarantees had been destroyed.

151

THE OBJECTION to war is not that it endangers human life,
but that it destroys human dignity. No enlightened man
would object to the occasional hemorrhage if we could
get rid of the moral indignation.

152

ANOTHER old punishment that might be profitably revived
is that of banishment. It actually survives, indeed, on certain lowly and surreptitious levels. The police magistrates
in the South not infrequently give a bad nigger twenty-four
hours to get out of town, and up to World War I magistrates everywhere sometimes ordered an unruly white youth
to enlist in the Navy. This last practise began to decay when
the Hon. Josephus Daniels undertook his historic effort to
convert the Navy into a branch of the Society of Christian

Endeavor. It is true that an order to a given misdemeanant to leave State A might be resented by the people of the adjoining States B, C and D, but it is not likely that any protest would follow if he were ordered to clear out of the United States. Canada would hardly notice a few additional ruffians, and Mexico might even welcome them.

153

HE IS not getting along so well. His competitors seem to be doing better. He formulates and begins to cherish the theory that he would be able to overhaul them if there were a change in the rules of the game, giving him a couple of marked cards. This is all that is to be found in nine-tenths of the fine schemes to lift up the lowly and make the world perfect. Coming from doctors who have no talent for their trade and see only the more ignorant and insolvent sort of patients, it is at the bottom of the demand that medicine be socialized. Coming from lawyers of the inferior moiety, with no rich and juicy clients, it has hatched the Lawyers Guild. Coming from aging police reporters, worn-out copy-readers and other such failures, it animates the Newspaper Guild. Coming from nations beaten in free competition by other nations, it produces the recurrent holy crusades to save democracy and put down sin.

154

THE DEMAND that labor unions be democratized is mere words, signifying nothing. Control of them must inevitably lie in the hands of professional politicians, just as control of the country must lie in the hands of other professional politicians. All the worst members—that is, all those who demand more and more money for less and less work— go to all meetings, make most of the speeches, and are ready with a majority whenever there is a vote. The more honest and intelligent members, after a little effort to oppose these frauds, see that it is hopeless and begin to stay away. The few who persist in opposition are then easily disposed of— by trumped-up fines, by the denial of opportunities to work, by constant objurgation, and by not infrequent threats of physical punishment. A union man of any sense is always a despairing fellow.

155

IT IS a curious fact that English (and American) physicists have always had a large hand in the attempt to reconcile science and theology—which always leads, of course, to science taking the short end of it. The names of Eddington, Jeans and Millikan suggest themselves at once, along with those of Kelvin, Lodge, Clerk-Maxwell and Faraday, not to mention Newton. Faraday was a member of a small and preposterous sect called Sandemanians, which practised foot-washing and other barbaric rites, and Lodge was a spiritualist. As for Newton, the greatest glory of English physics, he devoted more time and thought to theological speculation than to his proper business. This tendency to take theology seriously seems to be confined to the Anglo-Saxon physicists; there is little sign of it among their Continental colleagues, though some of the latter, notably Copernicus and Galileo, had to give a certain amount of lip service to the Roman demonology. Albert Einstein called attention to the English weakness in a sort of appendix to the American edition of Max Planck's "Where is Science Going?", published in 1933. "In England," he said, "there are scientific writers who are illogical and romantic in their popular writings, but in their scientific work they are acutely logical reasoners." He was hitting, obviously, at Jeans, who had argued that Planck's launching of the quantum theory had removed causation from the universe—a sheer imbecility. Unhappily, he made no attempt to explain this dichotomy, and it remains mysterious.

156

OF ALL varieties of men, the one who is least comprehensible to me is the fellow who immolates himself upon the altar of what he conceives to be the public interest—in other words, the reformer, the uplifter, the man, so-called, of public spirit. What I am chiefly unable to understand is his oafish certainty that he is right—his almost pathological inability to grasp the notion that, after all, he may be wrong. As for me, I am never absolutely certain that I am right, and for the plain reason that I am never absolutely certain that anything is true. It may *seem* to me to be true, and I may be quite unable to imagine any proof of its falsity—but that is simply saying that my imagination is limited, not that the proposition itself is immovably sound. Some other man, better born than I was or drinking better liquor, may disprove it tomorrow. And if not tomorrow, then day after tomorrow, or maybe next week, or next year. I know of no so-called truth that quite escapes this possibility. Anything is conceivable in a world so irrational as this one.

But even if the truth were not wobbly I should still

hesitate a long while before sacrificing any of my comfort or
security to it. The man who does so seems to me to be one
who deceives himself doubly. First, as I have noted, he convinces himself that he cannot be wrong, which is nonsense.
And then he convinces himself that he is disinterested, which
is also nonsense. Actually altruism simply does not exist on
earth, at least in our present glorious age. Even the most devoted nun, laboring all her life in the hospitals, is sustained
by the promise of a stupendous reward—in brief, billions of
centuries of undescribable bliss for a few years of unpleasant
but certainly not unendurable drudgery and privation.
What passes for altruism among lesser practitioners is even
less praiseworthy; in most cases, indeed, it is only too obviously selfish and even hoggish. In the case of the American
reformer, in his average incarnation, the motive seldom gets
beyond the yearning for power, the desire to boss things,
the itch to annoy his neighbors. If they really wanted to be
saved from their iniquities he would let them alone; if they
bawled to give up their money he would not press them for
it; if they did not flee him he would not pursue them. Well,
this happens to be a motive that burns in my own breast
very feebly, so I am not a reformer. Like all other men, of
course, I pant for power—but not the power to afflict and
dominate a rabble of my inferiors. I have had the job, in
the past, of bossing them, but it gave me no joy, and I got
rid of it as soon as possible. Thus I lack altogether the
messianic hankering, and to that extent must remain a bad
American. When people seem to me to be immersed in
error and sin, I can discover no impulse to save them, but
only a gentle hope that their follies will soon translate them

to bliss eternal, and I'll be rid of the nuisance of their presence.

157

THE RISE and fall of the New Humanism of Professor Irving Babbitt *et al* deserves a loving historian. It was launched by college bigwigs of the old-womanish type, and was mainly devoted to denouncing every approach to a realistic dealing with human life. The very thought of a physiological function sent Babbitt into a swoon. After his death and that of Paul Elmer More, the St. Louis, Mo., Plotinus, the young tutors who had been skipping and prancing after the flag began to fall off. Some of them became easy marks for the emerging Communists; the rest took to Christian Endeavor.

158

MULTITUDES of inferior men rejoice every time some new and bogus arcanum is announced. It offers them what seems to be an easy way out of their troubles, and when it fails to work, as it always does, their disappointment does not abate their appetite for more. The concept of the insoluble is simply beyond such poor fish, and doubt puts too great a strain upon their faculties. The early Christians were typical. They swallowed a long series of imbecilities against all the known evidence, and continued to believe in a Perusia long after every rational man laughed at it.

159

PATRIOTISM, though it is based upon the natural and indeed instinctive love of home, has been elevated in the modern world into an unparalleled congeries of imbecilities. What it demands of the individual citizen, as a practical matter, is that he yield not only his judgment but also his property and even his life to whatever gang of scheming politicians happen to be in power. The essence of his virtue as a patriot is that he ask no questions, once the band is set to playing.

160

THE INFLUENCE of the movies upon American *Kultur*, and even upon the general civilization of the world, has certainly been profound, but it has been still more profound upon the movie folk. They come, for the most part, from the lower orders, and whatever they learn of an urbane life on the movie lots is to them new and enchanting. Thus they tend to imitate in private the preposterous personages they enact on the screen. A movie actor's house, nine times out of ten, is a series of movie sets, and, like any other actor, he wears clothes that are hard to distinguish from his costumes. No movie gal believes that she has made the grade, socially speaking, until she has been through a succession of melodramatic domestic crises, usually ending in divorce. Her husbands, nearly always, are popinjays of the sort who have made love to her on the screen: she seldom tracks down and marries a man of any actual dignity. This is due in part, of course, to the fact that such men are usually suspicious of her, but that fact is not sufficient to account for the whole picture, for men of dignity have been known to succumb to even more meretricious hussies, and her social opportunities are enormously greater than those of any other ignorant woman. By the same token, it is most unusual for a movie actor to marry a woman of any genuine culture, or even of any marked decency. His wives are all shallow-pates, and most of them are forbiddingly shop-worn.

The movies are still in the Wild West stage of culture. They have yet to produce any authentic artists, for such an artist could not endure the kind of life nearly all movie people have to lead. The great magnates of the movie world would strike him precisely as a Hearst or a Harmsworth strikes a man of letters, or the sales agent of a phonograph company a composer of good music. It may be suggested here that perhaps Wagner was an exception—that he showed certain tastes that recall those of a movie star. But it must be manifest on reflection that there was actually a vast difference between the society of even a crazy king and that of a movie magnate, and an even vaster one between the atmosphere of Triebschen or Bayreuth, even with Cosima in the house, and that of Hollywood.

161

THE SUPERIORITY of the old-time American public school probably lay in the fact that it was operated on the master-and-apprentice system. The typical teacher was an educated young man who took a school to sustain himself while preparing for one of the professions. This system survived vestigially into my own time. The teacher who taught me most at the Polytechnic was Edward S. Kines, who paid for a course in law by playing pedagogue, and went to the bar as soon as the course was finished. When the American pedagogue became a professional, and began to acquire a huge armamentarium of technic, the trade of teaching de-

clined, for only inferior men were willing to undergo a long
training in obvious balderdash.

162

CONVERTING me to anything is probably a psychological
impossibility. At all events, it has never been achieved by
anyone, though I have been exposed more than once to the
missionary technic of very talented virtuosi. I can't recall
ever changing my mind about any capital matter. My general body of fundamental ideas is the same today as it was
in the days when I first began to ponder. I was never religious, and never a Socialist, even for a moment. My aver-
sion to conversion extends to other people: I always distrust and dislike a man who has changed his basic notions.
When a reader writes in to say that some writing of mine
has shown him the light and cured him of former errors I
feel disgust for him, and never have anything to do with
him if I can help it. I dislike, more or less, all Calvinists,
Communists and other such enemies of reason, but I dislike ex-Calvinists and ex-Communists very much more.

163

IDEAS of duty are mainly only afterthoughts. A young man
goes to war because he dislikes a dull job and craves one
that promises more excitement, or because he yearns to pos-
ture before his girl and the neighbors as a hero, or because
he has a sadistic itch to shoot someone, or because he is
ashamed to hold back while all the other boys are stepping
up, or because he is fetched by the press-gang and can't
help it, but if he returns alive he quickly picks up the con-

ventional assumption that patriotism is what moved him, and by the time he reaches middle age he is full of demands that all his successor youngsters imitate his public spirit.

164

WAR WILL never cease until babies begin to come into the world with larger cerebrums and smaller adrenal glands.

165

THE REV. clergy are the chief losers when such a quackery as the New Deal gets afoot. The sure-cure that it offers is appreciably better than the sure-cures that they offer. To be sure, it does not promise an eternity of bliss post-mortem, but the chances are that not many customers really take that promise at its face value, for it is hard to imagine even an idiot believing seriously that he will exist as a gaseous vertebrate for a hundred billion years. The prizes offered by political mountebanks are alike more plausible and more concrete, and hence more attractive. They meet immediate and highly conscious needs, and the clergy have nothing to match them. The American people do not go to revivals during a political campaign. They greatly prefer the Christmas presents promised by political mountebanks.

166

THE ELEMENTS in democracy that are sound in logic and of genuine cultural value may be very briefly listed. They are:

1. Equality before the law.
2. The limitation of government.
3. Free speech.

All the rest of the democratic dogma is, at best, dubious, and at worst palpable nonsense. No professional whooper-up of democracy, so far as I know, is in favor of the three things I have listed. Every time democratic enthusiasm rises to orgiastic heights violent attempts are made to put down all of them.

167

THE CHARM of the Confederates lies in the fact that they fought against heavy odds and carried on for four long years a war that was hopeless before the end of its first. They were the only Americans since the Revolution to show such gallantry and pertinacity. All other American wars have been fought with the odds overwhelmingly in favor of the Americans. They have suffered a few defeats—indeed, they have almost invariably suffered defeats when the odds were even or less—but they have never run any genuine risk of ultimate disaster. In the history of armed combat such affairs as the Mexican and Spanish-American wars must be ranked, not as wars at all, but as organized assassinations. In the two World Wars no American faced a bullet until his adversaries had been worn down by years of fighting others.

168

OF ALL human qualities, the one I admire most is competence. A tailor who is really able to cut and fit a coat seems to me to be an admirable man, and by the same token a university professor who knows little or nothing of the thing he presumes to teach seems to me to be a fraud and rascal. This explains my contempt for teachers of English:

not one in ten of them has any sort of grasp of the difficult subject he professes, or shows any desire to master it. The rest apparently proceed on the theory that English is something that every "educated" man knows, and that any such man is fit to teach it. It is actually full of subtleties and snares, as every professional writer of any capacity is well aware, and imparting it, if done effectively, must be very difficult. I suppose that the inferiority of the teachers of it is largely due to the fact that they are recruited from the lower moiety of pedagogical aspirants. The more ambitious fellows tackle something that seems more recondite, and hence better worth knowing. A prospective teacher of biology, say, or mathematics, or physics, cannot outfit himself for his career by reading a few plays of Shakespeare, memorizing the rules of grammar laid down by idiots, and learning to pronounce *either* as if it were spelled *eyether*; he must apply himself to a vast mass of strange and difficult facts, and mastering them requires a kind of capacity that is not common. The stupider fellow turns to something that is easier and more obvious, which is to say, to the language that every "educated" man is presumed to know, and the books he is presumed to have read. There is, of course, another factor, to wit, the need of many more teachers of English than any called for by any other subject. This excessive demand quickly exhausts all those who have any talent for it, and the dolts crowd in. More, they get a welcome, for in the absence of a sufficiency of competent teachers the syndics of educational institutions are forced to put up with second- and third-raters. They need fewer pedagogues in the other arts and sciences, and can thus pick and choose with more care. The effect of these varying demands is most shown in the field of so-called "education," where the training of multitudes of schoolma'ams calls for a faculty larger than nature can supply, with the result that a great many quacks get lodgment in it.

But in English even the higher ranks of professors tend to be inferior to those of any other faculty. The papers printed in the *English Journal*, the *Proceedings of the Modern Language Association* and similar periodicals seldom show any professional competence or contribute anything worth knowing to the subject. For the most part they consist wholly of dull pedantries—attempts to establish the dates of some forgotten poet, investigations of the stealings of one obscure author from another, elaborate statistical inquiries into weak endings, and so on and so on. The standards of professional research and writings in the United States are anything but high, but it would certainly be unusual to find any similar rubbish in a journal of chemistry, astronomy or zoology, or even in a medical journal. The men who actually know something always know the difference between something and nothing, but the professors of English seem to be largely unaware of it. They seldom tackle the really salient problems of their trade, for example, the nature and inner laws of the language they speak, or the ways and means of living writers of it. Instead, they devote themselves ardently to irrelevant trivia about the writers of the past, many of them existing today only as flies embalmed in the amber of text-books.

169

RELIGIOUS faith, even when it is sincere, does not always improve a man's conduct in his private relations. He may, for all his fear of Hell, remain a devious and unpleasant fellow, and his pious exercises may be no more than an effort to get into Heaven by false pretenses. It should be added, of course, that this is not always the case—that the fear of Hell may actually police him, and so make a better man of him. The Pennsylvania Dunkard who believes that God frowns upon debt is certainly a more appetizing neighbor than the Georgia sharecropper who believes that debt is one of God's ways of paying off His customers. He is a more industrious man and a far more useful citizen, though his fear of debt may make him unpleasantly avaricious, and indeed almost inhuman. But a money-grubbing Dunkard, at his worst, is far better than a sharecropper. He at least pulls his weight in the boat, and is not a burden on his neighbors.

170

THE THIRST for liberty does not seem to be natural to man. Most people want security in this world, not liberty. Liberty puts them on their own, and so exposes them to the natural consequences of their congenital stupidity and incompetence. Historically, it has always been forced upon the masses from above. Whenever they have formulated demands of their own, it has been demands for privileges, not for liberty.

171

THE EFFORT to explain away the Puritan, though it has been undertaken by earnest men and some of them have been more or less intelligent, has got nowhere. The facts are too plain to be disposed of by special pleading, however adroit. One of the favorite lines of approach is to demonstrate that the Puritan of New England was not altogether a savage— that he, too, had his *Kultur*, and that in part at least it was not inimical to civilization. This may be admitted, but it proves nothing. The Borgias also had their *Kultur*, and it was on a much higher level than that of the Puritans. So did the Victorian English. So did the Goths and Huns. So, also, there is a kind of *Kultur* in Serbia and Albania today, and even in Arkansas, Mississippi and Oklahoma. Nor is it apposite to show that the harsh mandates of the New England Puritans were never really enforced—that multitudes of antinomians resisted them from the first days, and that the Puritans themselves constantly evaded them. All this proves is that civilization survived, not because of Puritanism, but in spite of it. Nor is there any weight in pointing to the New England *Aufklärung*, for even a professional historian must be intelligent enough to see that it was a revolt *against* Puritanism. When that revolt began to succeed, the thing itself was driven into the South and West, and there it lingers today, uncontaminated by the flashes of enlightenment that ameliorated it in New England. Theologically speaking, rural Georgia is now in the state that Massachusetts was before 1787, when the first Unitarian church in Boston lit its fires; on other cultural counts it has hardly got beyond the Seventeenth Century, and in some ways it is actually in the Thirteenth. The defenders of Puritanism, it is to be noted, always confine their argument to New England, which is as absurd as confining an argument about Protestantism to Wittenberg. By 1800 it was actually weaker there than in any other area save the Southern Tidewater, and ever since then its stronghold has been elsewhere. The average American is no longer the average New Englander; he is rather the average Indianan, or Georgian, or Kansan. Scratch him, and you will find a Puritan.

172

THE ONLY way that democracy can be made bearable is by developing and cherishing a class of men sufficiently honest and disinterested to challenge the prevailing quacks. No such class has ever appeared in strength in the United States. Thus the business of harassing the quacks devolves upon the newspapers. When they fail in their duty, which is usually, we are at the quacks' mercy.

173

ALL THE leaders of groups tend to be frauds. If they were not, it would be impossible for them to retain the allegiance of their dupes. The executive secretary of an employers' organization is usually just as much a wind-bag and bunco-steerer as the head of a labor union. Both imitate the politicians who run every democratic country.

174

OF ALL the classes of men, I dislike most those who make their livings by talking—actors, clergymen, politicians, pedagogues, and so on. All of them participate in the shallow false pretenses of the actor who is their archetype. It is almost impossible to imagine a talker who sticks to the facts. Carried away by the sound of his own voice and the applause of the groundlings, he makes inevitably the jump from logic to mere rhetoric. His success is judged by the favor of his inferiors, or at all events of persons supposed to be his inferiors, and for that sort of thing I have no taste. If he is intelligent at all, which happens occasionally, he must be well aware that this favor is irrational and almost certainly transient. He is admired for his worst qualities, and he cannot count upon being admired for long. A good part of my time, in my earlier days, was spent in listening to speeches of one sort or another, and to watching their makers glow under the ensuing clapper-clawing. I was always sorry for such men, for I soon observed that the applause of today was almost invariably followed by the indifference of tomorrow. There is, indeed, no sadder man than a politician, providing, of course, he does not escape the usual fate of his order by a miracle. His eminence, while he lasts, is of a chiefly factitious variety, and has little relation, save perhaps an inverse one, to his merits. And his obscurity when his day is done is extraordinarily dark and dismal. The complaisant reflections that console other men are not for him. He cannot cherish his recollections of the applause of yesterday without painful thoughts of the lack of it today. There is seldom any residuum of permanent achievement in his memories. He is forgotten almost completely. He is dead all over. Grover Cleveland told the truth at the close of his second term as President. "The people," he said in effect, "are tired of me. They don't want to hear any more about me." For Cleveland there was some consolation in the continuing admiration of men he knew to be intelligent and unbiased, but for the average politico there is nothing.

175

So LONG as the Southern colleges have revivals on their campuses and students who get converted to Methodism and join the Y.M.C.A. are accepted as gentlemen, it will be impossible to think of the South as civilized. This is probably the chief difference between the Old South and the New. The educated folk of the Old took theology lightly, and religion to them was hardly more than a charming ritual, useful on solemn occasions. Such imbecilities as Methodism were patronized only by the lowly, whether white or black. Today, unhappily, they set the tone and color of Southern life, for the survivors of the old civilized minority have been driven underground. All forms of enlightenment, indeed, now lead an underground life below the Potomac. Notions that would be laughed at in the North even by policemen and trolley motormen are still taken gravely down there. A Protestant ecclesiastic, however ridiculous, gets polite notice from the newspapers, and even from the columnists thereof.

176

IN MY apprentice years as a literatus I made part of my living, like many others, as a dramatic critic for a daily newspaper. Compared to certain colleagues I was ignorant, but compared to the great majority, especially of old practitioners, I was extremely well-informed, and hence very cocky. Worse, I had a waggish pen, and knew how to make the readers of my paper snicker. This gift, exercised upon the poor mimes who frequented the town of my residence, frequently cast a blight upon the box-office, so the local Frohmans complained to my paper, and even demanded that I be cashiered forthwith. But the paper was so rich that I could afford to be virtuous, which is to say, unpleasant, and every time the Frohmans complained I simply threw on ten or twenty more amperes of my mockery, and drove a few more hundreds of possible patrons away from their houses. Finally, they gave it up. Then I tired of my job, and quit.

Who was right? I have no doubt today that the Frohmans were right. On the one hand stood a group of more or less reputable business men who had invested their money in a lawful and hazardous business, and were trying to make a living at it; on the other hand stood an irresponsible young man who deliberately tried to cut down their profits. I do not say that I was wrong about the plays and players they offered; on the contrary, I believe that I was usually right. But the essential thing is that I was absolutely without conscience or responsibility in the matter—that the worst that could have happened to me would have been the loss of my

job, and that this was very unlikely and I knew it to be unlikely—that, to all intents and purposes, I was engaged in a
combat in which my antagonists could and did suffer griev-
ous wounds, whereas I myself stood as secure against serious
injury as if I had been armed with Excalibur.

This was years ago, before experience of the world had
brought me sense, and before foreign travel had awakened
me to a consciousness of honor. I was young, and hence a
savage. But I often think of it today. And whenever I think
of it, the thought intrudes that this, fundamentally, is
what is the matter with the whole art of criticism: that
every critic is in the position, so to speak, of God, and has
no responsibility save to whatever may be visible of his own
decency. He can smite without being smitten. He challenges other men's work, and is exposed to no comparable
challenge of his own. The more reputations he breaks, the
more his own reputation is secured—and there is no lawful
agency to determine, as he himself professes to determine
in the case of other men, whether his motives are honest
and his methods are fair. Jahweh Himself is less irresponsible, for He at least must keep the respect of the theologians, or go down to ruin with His predecessors. But the
critic is judged only by public opinion—nay, by a very narrow and special opinion—and if he is a smart fellow, if he
really knows his trade, he is himself a chief influence in
forming that opinion.

177

MONEY is at least fifty times as valuable to a sick man as
to a well man. This is not because the rich patient gets

better medication than the poor man: in many cases, in fact, he gets worse. His advantage lies in the fact that he can be more comfortable when laid up, and has nothing save his actual illness to worry him.

178

THE COST of a parlor-car seat is the best investment open to an American. It gives him more for his money than anything else. He not only has a certain seat of his own, free from intrusion and reasonably roomy; he also rides in a car in which all of the people are clean and do not smell badly. The stinks in a day-coach, even under the best of circumstances, are revolting. The imbecile conversation that goes on in parlor-car smoke-rooms is sometimes hard to bear, but there is escape from it in one's seat; the gabble in day-coaches is worse, and it is often accompanied by all sorts of other noises. But the main thing is that parlor-car passengers, white or black, do not smell like wild animals. Some of them, perhaps, are naturally dirty, but when they take a Pullman seat they have washed and are in their Sunday clothes.

179

THE HUMAN race has probably never produced a wholly admirable man. Such trite examples as Lincoln, Washington, Goethe and the holy saints are obviously very lame candidates. Even Jesus fails to meet any rational specification. His stupendous ignorance must be obvious even to Christians, for His false assumptions were gross and innumerable. He was probably dirty in person and He was certainly superstitious, for he believed in devils. There were many better men in the Palestine of His time, but certainly there was none good enough to be called with any sense a perfect man. Such a prodigy is perhaps forever unrealizable.

180

THE SUPERIOR intelligence of women seems to be incompatible with their ready yielding to hideous and silly fashions, but is it really? I suspect that dressing up absurdly may be only their way of escape from the harshness and dullness of their daily lives, which are enormously less rich, varied and entertaining than those of men. A few women in the arts attain to a degree of freedom and self-realization comparable to that of men, but on the lower levels where most women have to remain they fall far short of anything of the sort. A woman of the highest order of intelligence, entering into the sciences, or into commerce or manufacturing, always finds herself subordinate to some man, and it not infrequently happens that he is her inferior on all rational counts. It is, indeed, a commonplace of observation that some of the largest of American enterprises are actually run, not by the male magnificoes who get all the glory, but by their female secretaries. Personal adornment offers such women their only public means of exercising their egos, and when they make it unsightly it is perhaps only a sorry device for making it arresting. The same tendency toward the ugly and the unseemly is also visible in frustrated types of men—for example, the Shriner who arrays himself in a Turkish fez and parades obscenely in the hot sun, or the

Rotarian who finds a high solace in calling a bishop Charlie or in blowing spit-balls at a United States Senator.

181

WHAT is the function that a clergyman performs in the world? Answer: he gets his living by assuring idiots that he can save them from an imaginary hell. It is a business almost indistinguishable from that of a seller of snake-oil for rheumatism. As for a lawyer, he is simply, under our cash-register civilization, one who teaches scoundrels how to commit their swindles without too much risk. As for a physician, he is one who spends his whole life trying to prolong the lives of persons whose deaths, in nine cases out of ten, would be a public benefit. The case of the pedagogue is even worse. Consider him in his highest incarnation: the university professor. What is his function? Simply to pass on to fresh generations of numskulls a body of so-called knowledge that is fragmentary, unimportant, and, in large part, untrue. His whole professional activity is circumscribed by the prejudices, vanities and avarices of his university trustees, *i.e.*, a committee of soap-boilers, nail-manufacturers, bank-directors and politicians. The moment he offends these vermin he is undone. He cannot so much as think aloud without running a risk of having them fan his pantaloons.

182

THE SUPER-PEDAGOGUES use schoolma'ams in their grandiose and quackish operations just as the politicians who operate nations use soldiers. "Theirs not to reason why; theirs but to do or die." If one of them, showing intelligence, revolts against the prevailing mumbo-jumbo she is punished almost as brutally as a soldier evading service in time of war. There is something pathetic about both the soldier and the school-ma'am. They have laborious jobs, and their rewards are very meagre. Whenever a given school system turns out to be relatively rational and effective, no one remembers the ma'ams who make it so, for all the credit and glory are hogged by the super-gogues at the head of it. And when another school system is discovered to be intolerantly in-effective the blame is heaped on the ma'ams, and the super-gogues proceed to supplant them with others trained in some new abracadabra. These successive revelations are al-most unanimously preposterous. To be sure, there have been some advances in the art of teaching the young during the past century, but they have been far from numerous, and most of them have been put into effect at the demand of parents, not on the motion of professional pedagogues. The latter have incommoded the schoolma'am much more than they have aided her, and when she succeeds at her dismal task it is usually in spite of them, not because of them. It is still an open question whether the pedagogical methods of today are better or worse than those prevailing in the little red schoolhouse of the past generations, and many intelligent persons believe that they are clearly worse. There is certainly no such doubt about the improvement of methods, say, in medicine, farming or the common me-chanical processes.

183

ON SOME bright tomorrow, so I hope and pray, someone will write a history of common sense. The gradual develop-

ment of the prevailing metaphysical, political, theological
and economic delusions has been recorded in a vast series of
books, but no one has ever thought to record the evolution
of the sort of wisdom that really keeps human society a
going concern. I'd certainly like to know, if it can be found
out, who was the first man to doubt the magic of priests,
and likewise who was the first to note the vanity of all so-
called philosophical speculation. These fellows were enormous benefactors of mankind, and yet they are as completely forgotten as the lost inventors of the plow, the
boat and the wheel. They were the real begetters of everything properly describable as sound information and rational
thinking. Their ribald hoots were worth the soaring fancies
of all the sages, and ten thousand times as much. Every
time anyone says anything worth hearing today it goes back
to them, and every time a new fallacy is launched it is in
contempt of them.

But would it be a service to their names to dig them
up, resuscitate them, print them? Maybe not. The human
race, taking one day with another, has very little respect for
intelligence; what it really admires is presumption, effron-
tery, dogmatism. Its greatest heroes, at least in the domain
of ideas, have always been enemies of the plain fact. Consider, for example, the undisputed master theologian of the
Western World, to wit, Paul of Tarsus: his basic doctrines,
reduced to plain English, become indistinguishable from
those of a Tennessee Fundamentalist. If it had not been
for the revolt of common sense against him we'd still be
trying to speak in the tongues and to cure warts with prayer.

184

WHAT is commonly described as racial or religious prejudices is sometimes only a reasonable prudence. At the bottom of it there is nothing more wicked than a desire to
prevent dominance by a strange and more or less hostile
minority. This was true, certainly, of the old animosity to
the Irish Catholics, and it is true again of much American
anti-Semitism. In the South it is even true, at least to some
extent, of the violent feeling against the Negro.

185

I SEE no objection to letting young college tutors and other
such pedagogues follow the Communist party line. Whatever such simpletons teach becomes abhorrent and incredible to their pupils. Their teaching of arithmetic has
widely prospered the idea that two and two may equal five.
Their teaching of literature has made the comic strip a
national art form. Their teaching of music has made jazz
another. Their teaching of history has established the radio
commentator.

186

COLLEGE football would be much more interesting if the
faculty played instead of the students, and even more interesting if the trustees played. There would be a great increase in broken arms, legs and necks, and simultaneously
an appreciable diminution in the loss to humanity.

187

NOTHING could be more absurd than the common Southern doctrine that the Negro's best friend is the Southerner. It is, of course, a fact that there is a minority of Southerners who sincerely wish him well, but it does not include the vast horde of crackers. Moreover, every Southerner, however enlightened, is likely to turn cracker when hard pushed. So far he will go in granting rights and privileges to his colored brother, but no further. No Southerner, save an occasional fanatic like Lillian Smith, author of "Strange Fruit," has ever argued seriously that intermarriage between the races should be tolerated. Even in the North partisans who go so far are rare, and most of them are obvious psychopaths. Very few of the more vocal Negrophils are uncontaminated by self-interest. If they are black themselves, they are almost unanimously exploiters, and if they are white they are usually politicians, including Communists. Really disinterested well-wishers, with absolutely nothing to sell, are rare indeed. Thus the poor blackamoor is thrown upon his own, and whatever progress he makes toward full citizenship must be engineered by himself. In the end, I suppose, the law of natural selection will decide the matter, as it always does in this world. To advocate submission to it always sets the tin-horn messiahs to howling, but there it stands none the less. The best the Negro can do is to make his immediate situation as tolerable as possible. This he commonly does with great skill. He is an adept at hoodwinking the whites, and seems to get a great deal of fun out of the process. A large part of Negro talk consists of poking fun at white people. Save among the professional race-savers, there is even enough humor in the race to make it laugh at his own difficulties.

188

THE LOGICAL pull in favor of monarchy is constantly visible in the United States. We have discovered by long experience that it is desirable to put the head of the state above politics. He is surely not so in fact, but nevertheless we have developed a convention which assumes that he is. Evidences of it are the recurrent cries to support the President in emergencies, and the gradual growth of taboos which protect him from the more effective sorts of criticism. It becomes an indecorum to denounce him openly in Congress, yet he remains an active politician all the while. Our system of bringing him to book is an extremely clumsy one, and the English scheme for dealing with the Prime Minister is obviously very much better. To be sure, the Prime Minister need not answer the questions put to him in the Commons, but his very failure to do so is a kind of answer in itself, and may cost him his job.

189

IT SEEMS to be the common belief in the United States that a new factory is a valuable acquisition to a city or town, and that any man who sets up one is a public benefactor. The local Rotarians and other such imbeciles always give him a hearty welcome, and not infrequently he is accorded substantial tax exemptions. In the days following Reconstruction many of the one-horse cotton-mills that still afflict the South were built by public subscription, and large subscribers were honored as notable philanthropists. This delusion raged all over America in the high days of the Coolidge prosperity and was revived during World War II. In consequence many an otherwise peaceful and charming town was polluted and ruined; indeed, there was scarcely a town in the country that did not suffer more or less damage. The injury to Baltimore was large and palpable. The new factories opened in boom days brought in hordes of low-grade labor, and the result was a marked decline in the average intelligence and decency of the population. During World War II the effect was even worse, for nearly all the strangers recruited to man the war plants were either hill-billies from Appalachia or lintheads from the more languishing Southern mill-towns. These newcomers propagated disease, filled the public schools with their filthy progeny, kept the police jumping, and wrecked whole neighborhoods. Of the 250,000 or more, white and black, who came in first and last probably not more than 200 were of any value as citizens. They were, in fact, so uniformly inferior that even the constructive thinkers who at first hailed them ended by praying to a sportive and unjust God that they would quickly return home. The patriotic entrepreneurs who afflicted Baltimore with these revolting morons made no contribution whatever to civilization in the town. Some of them set up as civic leaders, made endless speeches and whooped up all sorts of costly and idiotic "improvements," but they never had anything worth hearing to say, and not many of them returned in taxes the extra expense they laid on the community. The cost of one of them, Glenn L. Martin, the airship manufacturer, must have run to many millions, but the values the

city got out of him were precisely nil. One S. Teackle Wallis
or Richard M. Venable was worth more than a whole herd
of such fellows.

190

THERE seems to be a deep instinct in women which teaches
them that most of the aspirations of men are vain. They
seem to know that, of a multitude of starters in the race,
only a few can ever succeed—and that most of the few are
miserable both along the way and at the goal. Progress, indeed, is almost always attained at the cost of human happiness. The majority of men, like nearly all women, prefer
ease and security to high ambition and arduous enterprise.
They prefer domestic peace and comfort to public acclaim
—or execration.

191

WHAT broke down democracy at last was precisely what
was most rational in it—for example, the heavy stressing of
self-reliance, the doctrine of equality before the law, government by laws not men, the insistence upon free competition. All these things turned out to be abhorrent to the
majority of idealistic Americans, which is to say, to the majority of poor fish. The New Deal was certainly not the
first revolt against them. That revolt began so long ago as
Jefferson's time, and it has been rolling up ever since.

192

ONE READS constantly, in the writings of such latter-day
Pascals and Butlers as Millikan and Eddington, that science has failed as a guide of mankind—that there is a thirst

in the human psyche which it cannot assuage. This is simply pious nonsense. It may be true for many men, and perhaps even for the overwhelming majority of men, but it is certainly not true for all. I offer myself as an example. To me the scientific point of view is completely satisfying, and it has been so as long as I can remember. Not once in this life have I ever been inclined to seek a rock and a refuge elsewhere. It leaves a good many dark spots in the universe, to be sure, but not a hundredth time as many as theology. We may trust it, soon or late, to throw light upon many of them, and those that remain dark will be beyond illumination by any other agency. It also fails on occasion to console, but so does theology; indeed, I am convinced that man, in the last analysis, is intrinsically inconsolable. All that Eddington and Millikan achieve, when they attempt their preposterous reconciliation of science and theology, is to prove that they themselves, for all their technical skill, are scientists only by trade, not by conviction. They practise science diligently and to some effect, but only in the insensate way in which Blind Tom played the piano. The dead hand is on them, and they can't get rid of a congenital credulity. Science, to them, remains a bit strange and shocking. They are somewhat in the position of a Christian clergyman who finds himself unable to purge himself of a suspicion that Jonah, after all, probably did *not* swallow the whale.

193

THE MOST expensive thing on this earth is to believe in something that is palpably not true. The burden of quackery has never been properly estimated. The early Christians sold their property and abandoned their families in confidence that the end of the world was at hand. There was no evidence for this save the assurance of the quacks who operated upon them. The quacks got enormous power out of the process, and in all probability cabbaged most of their victims' property. The victims themselves acquired nothing save the hope of reward post-mortem, which was, of course, hollow and vain. To this day the rewards that political quacks offer are quite as valueless.

194

THE LOSS of faith, to many minds, involves a stupendous upset—indeed, that upset goes so far in some cases that it results in something hard to distinguish from temporary insanity. It takes a long while for a naturally trustful person to reconcile himself to the idea that after all God will not help him. He feels like a child thrown among wolves. For this reason I have always been chary about attempting to shake religious faith. It seems to me that the gain to truth that it involves is trivial when set beside the damage to the individual. To be sure, he is also improved, but he is almost wrecked in the process.

195

WE HAVE no really effective political opposition in this country. The minority in Congress is always easily intimidated. Moreover, the professional interests of its members are identical with those of the majority. All politicians are eager to spend as much money as possible, and to create as many jobs as possible. The Republican politicians of the

1933–45 era did not really object to the multiplication of jobholders under Roosevelt II. What they always had in mind was not the looting of the taxpayer, but the probability that soon or late they'd have a multitude of jobs to fill themselves. The war on such extravagance and waste must be carried on by other agencies.

196

NEXT to the ant and the bee man seems to be the most social of animals. Certainly no other mammal approaches him here. He can scarcely think of himself as an individual: in his own mind he is always a member of some group. Naturally enough, he tries to join a group that is somehow distinguished, and hence capable of increasing his feeling of importance. This is why people try to get into what is called good society, and into clubs and other organizations that pretend to exclusiveness. On lower levels there are thousands of such outfits, ranging from college fraternities and the Shriners at the top to the Ku Klux Klan and the Red Men at the bottom. Membership in Rotary, to the sort of man who becomes a Rotarian, is a very valuable distinction. Once in, he can look down on the Kiwanians, who stand upon the next lower step and look down in their turn upon the Lions, Optimists and other such poor fish. There is an order of rank in the fraternal orders, well marked and well understood. An Elk is superior to an Eagle, who is superior to a Moose. A Freemason, however lowly, believes that he is above, and is generally admitted to be above, an Odd Fellow or a Knight of Pythias. It is hard to find an American who doesn't claim membership in some such group. All have the common end of making the joiner feel important, and, in some way or other, powerful. The stress laid on secrecy by many of them has the same purpose. The secrets of the Freemasons and their imitators have been printed often, and on inspection they turn out to be idiotic, yet the moron admitted to them officially always feels a sharp enhancement of his personality.

197

GOVERNMENT, like any other organism, refuses to acquiesce in its own extinction. This refusal, of course, involves the resistance to any effort to diminish its powers and prerogatives. There has been no organized effort to keep government down since Jefferson's day. Ever since then the American people have been bolstering up its powers and giving it more and more jurisdiction over their affairs. They pay for that folly in increased taxes and diminished liberties. No government as such is ever in favor of the freedom of the individual. It invariably seeks to limit that freedom, if not by overt denial, then by seeking constantly to widen its own functions.

198

OF ALL Christian dogmas, perhaps the most absurd is that of the Atonement, for it not only certifies to the impotence of God but also to His lack of common sense. If He is actually all-wise and all-powerful then He might have rescued man from sin by devices much simpler and more rational than the sorry one of engaging in fornication with a young peasant girl, and then commissioning the ensuing love-child to save the world. And if He is intelligent, He would have chosen a far more likely scene for the business than an obscure corner of the Roman empire, among a people of no influence or importance. Why not Rome itself? Why was not Jesus sent there, instead of being confined to the back alleys of Palestine? His followers, after His execution, must have asked themselves something like this question, for they proceeded at once upon the missionary journeys that He had never undertaken Himself. Their success was only moderate, for they were men of despised castes, and the doctrine they preached was quickly corrupted by borrowings from the various other cults of the time and from their own ignorant speculations. Indeed, the whole machinery of propaganda was managed so clumsily that Christianity prevailed at last by a series of political accidents, none of them having anything to do with its fundamental truth. Even so, the overwhelming majority of human beings remained unaffected by it, and it was more than a thousand years before so many as half of them had heard of it. During all this time, by Christian theory, they remained plunged in the sins that Jesus was sent to obliterate, and countless multitudes of them must have gone to Hell. To this day there are many millions still in that outer darkness, including all the Moslem nations, all the great peoples of Asia, and nearly all the savages on earth. Certainly, it would be impossible to imagine a more inept and ineffective scheme for saving humanity. It was badly planned, its execution was left mainly to extremely stupid men, and it failed to reach all save a minute minority of the men and women it was designed for. I can think of no human reformer, not clearly insane, who has managed his propaganda so badly.

199

I HOPE no one will mistake my occasional animadversions on the English for moral indignation. They are, in their international relations, scoundrels, but so are all other nations. If they differ from the rest it is only in the superior impudence and shamelessness of their false pretenses, the immeasurably greater virulence of their hypocrisy. This, it seems to me, is a kind of superiority. I respect a clever thief more than I respect a bungling one. Even among theologians there are differences flowing out of relative virtuosity. A man who does well whatever he undertakes to do is surely not to be sniffed at.

200

KIPLING in his early verse made an attempt to glorify the game of grab of the English imperialists, and it was largely successful. What was at bottom only a mercenary trading venture began to take on an almost heroic guise. In the same way Whitman attempted to glorify the American democracy of his time. The actual democracy of 1875 was an extraordinarily degraded and ignominious thing, just as the British imperialism of 1900 was degraded and ignominious. World War I exposed Kipling. He responded by throwing off his noble disguise and showing all the moral indignation of an alarmed patriot. His poetry thus ceased to sooth and enchant, and the English themselves became ashamed of him. A creative artist always comes to ruin when he begins to defend the reigning demagogues.

2 0 1

MANKIND has failed miserably in its effort to devise a rational system of government. Some of the best intellects the race has produced have tackled the problem, for example, Aristotle, Hobbes and Locke, but they have all failed. Perhaps they have failed largely because they have not resorted to the lowly weapon of common sense. Government does not present an esoteric problem, but a highly practical problem. If that problem is ever solved it will not be by metaphysicians, but by hard-boiled men. My belief is that the nearest approach to a solution that is conceivable will have to be provided by something on the order of a world conqueror. If a really first-rate man got control of all Europe he could vastly improve the government of every country, and immensely diminish its cost. Unfortunately, such a man could achieve only a transient reform. The inevitability of his own death would work against him during his lifetime, and on his actual exitus there would be a battle royal, with a probable return to all the imbecilities of nationalist particularism. In brief, the problem is probably forever insoluble. Very few men are actually eager for the durable good of the world, and none of those who are attain to political power. The art of government is the exclusive possession of quacks and frauds. It has been so since the earliest days, and it will probably remain so until the end of time.

2 0 2

I MARVEL that no one tries to launch a royalist movement in the United States. I have printed several articles in favor of it from time to time, but they were always more or less jocose. Nine Americans out of ten are actually monarchists at bottom. The fact is proved by their high susceptibility to the political claims of presidents' sons and other relatives, usually nonentities. The rise of Roosevelt II was obviously due to his name. He would never have been appointed Assistant Secretary of the Navy if it had not been for that name—indeed, he would never have been elected to the New York State Senate. Wilson appointed him to the Navy Department for the same reason that Roosevelt I appointed Charles J. Bonaparte—in order to gather in some reflected dynastic glory.

203

PROBABLY the only decent government ever heard of in South America was the one set up by the Jesuits in Paraguay. It would be interesting to inquire into the consequences of its collapse. While it existed Paraguay was well governed and life was safe, but as soon as it fell there followed a bath of blood. The totalitarian paternalism of the Jesuits apparently fitted South American conditions enormously better than democracy. Nevertheless, democratic theory prevailed, and the whole of Latin America has been racked by turmoil and corruption ever since.

204

THE MAIN thing that every political campaign in the United States demonstrates is that the politicians of all parties, despite their superficial enmities, are really members of one great brotherhood. Their principal, and indeed their sole, object is to collar public office, with all the privileges and profits that go therewith. They achieve this collaring by buying votes with other people's money. No professional politician is ever actually in favor of public economy. It is his implacable enemy, and he knows it. All professional politicoes are devoted wholeheartedly to waste and corruption. They are the enemies of every decent man.

205

I AM one of the few *Goyim* who have ever actually tackled the Talmud. I suppose you now expect me to add that it is a profound and noble work, worthy of hard study by all other *Goyim*. Unhappily, my report must differ from this expectation. It seems to me, save for a few bright spots, to be quite indistinguishable from rubbish. If, at its highest, it is genuinely worth reading, then at its lowest it is on all fours with the Koran, "Science and Health" and the Book of Mormon.

206

THE IDEA at the bottom of the Christian eucharist is precisely the idea at the bottom of cannibalism. That is to say, the devotee believes that he will acquire something of the psychological quality of the creature by devouring its body. All the metaphysical adornments of that plain fact are afterthoughts. They did not appear until after skeptics had begun to expose the true inwardness of the rite.

207

FEW MEMBERS of Congress, in either House, are men of any genuine distinction. Even the lawyers who swarm there are, with very few exceptions, bad ones, and the height of their advocacy has been reached in advocating jobs for themselves. Whatever eminence a congressman really enjoys in the world is derived directly and usually solely from his seat. The minute he loses it he resumes his earlier character of nonentity. This fact was noted by Tocqueville so long ago as 1835. It has not changed since.

208

Some of the most anti-social of crimes still go unpunished by our archaic and preposterous laws. So far as I know, it is not a criminal offense in any American State to beget a syphilitic child. Its care throws a heavy burden on the taxpayer, and its life is one long misery, but its father and mother, though in most cases they beget it knowingly, are not punished. I'd like to hear argument, in the cases where they do so knowingly, against putting them to death.

209

Some time ago I went to a dinner at Washington attended by many high politicoes and a large number of the newspapermen who write about them. I was struck forcibly by the fact that most of those politicoes were strangers to me, whereas most of the newspapermen were old friends. The politician is the most transient of the world's great men. Who knows who was Speaker of the House under Hayes? Or Secretary of the Navy under Taft? Such nonentities, thrown into positions of great power and glamor, appear to the common run to be really first-rate, but they are mainly only third-raters, and they prove it by their lack of durability. Not many of them last.

2 1 0

ONE OF the amusing by-products of war is its pricking of the fundamental democratic delusion. For years *Homo boobus* stalks the earth vaingloriously, flapping his wings over his God-given rights, his inalienable freedom, his sublime equality to his masters. Then of a sudden he is thrust into a training camp, and discovers that he is a slave, after all— that even his life is not his own. One day he is the favorite of the Constitution and the peer of George Washington. The next day he is standing in line with a musket over his shoulder, and an officer is barking at him.

2 1 1

THE IDEA that the only alternative is between democracy on the one side and some sort of totalitarianism on the other is hardly tenable. Any reflective man could easily imagine better systems. The essential problem is plain enough. It is to set up a government that will retain control by relatively enlightened and decent people, and yet work equal justice to the inferior. Experience with democracy has proved that giving the inferior power always impedes this equal justice. They not only deny it to their superiors, they even deny it to each other—indeed, the concept of equal justice is essentially aristocratic, and entertaining it seems to be impossible to the inferior varieties of man. Their needs are so desperate that they can think of nothing else. Every time they yield anything to the man above them they must lose something that they believe to be essential. The old platitude that only the rich can be generous is true in the field of privilege as well as in the field of money. The man who is completely free is usually willing to give some of his freedom to others, and even the most violent despots in human history have sometimes shown that tendency. But the nether herd never shows it. Whenever it has the power to oppress its betters it always uses that power, and usually in a brutal manner. Popular revolutions are invariably marked by gross excesses. It is sometimes overlooked that revolutions of the ballot often show just as much excess as those of the bullet. The plain people, having won an election, are merciless to those who lose it. It is only the moderating influence of the upper classes that keeps them from bitter and ruinous reprisals.

Here the influence of the class of professional politicians probably works for the good. Though they are unanimously scoundrels they are at least more foresighted than the mob, and those on the opposite sides maintain amicable personal relations. Thus they are reluctant to punish each other too violently, and so the great body of non-political persons escapes. This fact may be one of the considerations to be urged in favor of democracy. In other words, it may be tolerable simply because the politicians who operate it are cynics. They never quite believe in the great causes that they merchant to the plain people, nor do they ever quite believe in the infamy of the opposition. The plain people are always outraged when they discover evidences of this tolerance, just as an ignorant litigant is outraged when he sees his lawyer eating lunch with the lawyer of his oppo-

nent. But it is precisely such cynicism toward undying doctrines and holy causes that makes civilized life possible in
the world.

212

WHO WILL argue that 98.6 Fahrenheit is the right tempera-
ture for man? As for me, I decline to do it. It may be that
we are all actually freezing: hence the pervading stupidity
of mankind. At 110 or 115 degrees even archbishops might
be intelligent.

213

THE MORE noisy Negro leaders, by depicting all whites as
natural and implacable enemies to their race, have done it
a great disservice. Large numbers of whites who were
formerly very friendly to it, and willing to go to great
lengths to help it, are now resentful and suspicious. The
effort to purge the movies, the stage, the radio and the
comic-strips of the old-time Negro types has worked the
same evil. The Negro comic character may have engendered
a certain amount of amiable disdain among whites, but he
certainly did not produce dislike. We do not hate people
we laugh at and with. His chief effect upon white thinking,
in fact, was to spread the idea that Negroes as a class are
very amiable folk, with a great deal of pawky shrewdness.
This was to their advantage in race relations. But when the
last Amos 'n' Andy programme is suppressed the Negro,
ceasing to be a charming clown, will become a menacing
stranger, and his lot will be a good deal less comfortable
than it used to be.

214

THE SOCIAL worker, judging her by her own pretensions, helps to preserve multitudes of persons who would perish if left to themselves. Thus her work is clearly dysgenic and anti-social. For every victim of sheer misfortune that she restores to self-sustaining and social usefulness, she must keep alive scores of misfits and incompetents who can never, for all her help, pull their weight in the boat. Such persons can do nothing more valuable than dying.

215

IT IS always dangerous to make doing good a source of power and profit, and usually disastrous. This is shown plainly in the case of the American public schools, which are founded upon the altruistic doctrine that even the poorest child deserves a sound education, but have degenerated into self-seeking camorras of incompetent and unconscionable pedagogues. The truth is that in any conflict between altruistic purpose and private self-interest the latter always wins hands down. It wins, indeed, the instant the two come into contact.

216

I SEE devotion all about me, and for the thing itself have a certain amount of respect. It at least tends toward unselfishness, even when it is not unselfish in origin. Unhappily, it is nearly always wasted upon false gods. The thing I have tried to preach is simply homage to facts, clear and free thinking, intellectual decency. To be sure, my own experience has taught me how difficult that is, but nevertheless I believe that a steady effort to attain it should be made at all times and everywhere. The man who tries and fails is unfortunate, but he is certainly not contemptible. But how many men really try? Probably not one in a thousand. The rest simply embrace delusions, and so nine-tenths of the devotion of mankind is wasted upon obvious imbecilities.

217

It used to be believed that Germans were narrow specialists; indeed, that charge was frequently made during World War I by the idiots who specialized in German infamy. The record, of course, runs the other way. The cases of Herder, Leibniz and Goethe come to mind at once. It has been said, and with some justice, that Goethe was the first *general* man since Leonardo da Vinci. Many other examples could be cited. Ostwald, the great chemist, was also a highly competent theologian; Virchow was a politician of wide capacity and influence; Billroth was an excellent musician and the best friend of Brahms; Wagner wrote both the words and music of his music dramas, and also did a great many theoretical works.

218

The confusion and absurdity in the current discussion of democracy are largely produced by the error of thinking of the franchise as a right; it is actually a privilege. When it is thought of as a right it must be granted arbitrarily and without discrimination, and the result is a series of situations that war with all sense. By what process does a young man or woman become competent to vote at the precise age

of twenty-one? The answer, of course, is that no such process can be demonstrated, even statistically; it is purely imaginary. Plenty of Americans, and perhaps a majority, are too
stupid at twenty-five, or thirty-five, or even forty-five to vote
with anything properly describable as intelligence, and large
numbers of those who are apparently smart enough are too
dishonest to do so conscientiously. These fools and rogues
are the natural meat of demagogues, and in the average
election they probably determine the result. Indeed, it
would not be going too far to say that they almost invariably determine it. Thus the whole device of taking votes is
reduced to nonsense, and persons who favor it as it stands
are thrown back upon the mystical theory that the ignorant
and knavish, when they go into the polling-place, are guided
by something indistinguishable from divine inspiration.
This theory is at the bottom of the often heard contention
that the plain people, in the long run, always decide great
questions wisely. It is possible that this actually happens,
but if so the wise decision usually comes at the end of a
long succession of unwise ones, and it is seldom possible to
demonstrate a really intelligent process in the steps by
which it is finally reached. Normally, the plain people vote
irrationally and at random, and when sound sense eventually emerges (which it certainly doesn't do invariably)
the result is statistical rather than rational.

The doctrine that every legal adult, save only the insane and unpardoned felons, should be given one vote has
hardened into such rigid dogma in the United States that
it is seldom subjected to reasonable examination and discussion. To question it, even by indirection, has become a

kind of crime. Yet it is easy to imagine voting systems that would be infinitely more plausible. As for me, I have long believed that the franchise should be something earned by socially useful conduct, not acquired by the mere passage of time. Why should a wholly stupid and incompetent man or woman be permitted to vote at any time, soon or late? It would be quite as rational to give the franchise to children of eighteen, as has been actually proposed, or even to children of sixteen, or fourteen, or twelve. It would be much wiser to withhold it until the right to it has been demonstrated by objective evidence. I believe that any man or woman who, for a period of say five years, has earned his or her living in some lawful and useful occupation, without any recourse to public assistance, should be allowed to vote, and that no one else should be allowed to vote. I believe the definition of a useful occupation should be as wide as possible, even at the cost of giving one class of voters an advantage over other classes. This inequality of power, in truth, is inseparable from the democratic process. We have it now, but with the difference that the balance of power tends to fall into the hands of a class that is not useful at all. After all, why should not the majority of decent, self-sustaining and self-respecting persons dominate the country? I can discover no reason—at least so long as the theory is entertained that government is an agency of the people. What we need to get rid of, if possible, is its control by a majority that is human only biologically, and hence cannot be trusted to determine wisely the best interests of the country, or even, indeed, its own best interests. The loutish

mob now in control, succumbing constantly to unconscionable demagogues, not only exposes the rest of us to recurrent damage and even catastrophe; it also works steadily
against its own ultimate welfare. Deceived by the promise
of Utopia tomorrow, it heads inevitably into slavery hereafter.

The best test of a free citizen, it seems to me, is his
capacity to pull his weight in the boat. If he shows that
he can't do so I see no reason why he should be permitted
to share the earnings and regulate the conduct of those
who can. The question whether his incapacity is due to
laziness, to some congenital defect or to sheer ill luck is
essentially irrelevant. The important thing is that he has
failed as a man, and hence can't be imagined succeeding
as a citizen. Save in the case of sheer ill luck he has abundantly demonstrated his inferiority, and no good can be got
out of inquiring into its causes. *Res ipsa loquitur.* Even in
the case of clearly apparent ill luck I see no injustice in
keeping him waiting until his luck changes, or he surmounts
it, for unlucky men are usually bitter men, with a strong
tendency to envy and hate the lucky. Giving them a franchise to determine the rights and duties of the lucky is as
clearly irrational as it would be to let blind men make laws
for the seeing. The fate of all of us is determined, in the
last analysis, by fortune. It provides our opportunities in
this world, and fixes our rewards and punishments. Why
should a man whom fortune is plainly against be entitled
to wreak his vengeance on those whom fortune more or
less favors? The common answer to this question is based

on sentimentality, not on reason. It is responsible for all of the looting and skulduggery that go on in the name of democracy.

219

CAPITAL punishment has probably been responsible for a good deal of human progress. The sentimental theory that in the England of the days of wholesale hangings a great many innocent persons were put to death, and a great many others who were superior and valuable, is not borne out by the known evidence. The good and the superior seldom went to the gallows—the former because it was impossible, even under the harsh laws then prevailing, to pin crimes on them, and the latter because they were too smart. Thus the overwhelming majority of those executed were of the sort whose departures for bliss eternal improved the average intelligence and decency of the race. They left the earth, to paraphrase the shrewd John Gay, for the earth's good.

220

NOTHING of any permanent good can be done for the man who is stupid and lazy and has too many children. He was the chief beneficiary of the New Deal, but despite all the billions spent upon him his condition after World War II was as bad as it had been in 1932. In brief, keeping him alive never shows any net profit. He can be lifted up transiently, but he always slips back again. What is worse, he pulls a good man with him every time. It would be interesting to estimate the number of children born to such vermin during the twelve years of Roosevelt II. They probably produced four or five millions. Of these poor wretches fully a half are now fit for nothing save following in their fathers' footsteps. The New Deal was probably the most stupendous dysgenic enterprise ever undertaken by man. It not only cost the American taxpayer billions and greatly depleted the accumulated resources of the country; it also burdened future generations with a charge that will grow larger and larger as year chases year. If Roosevelt's colossal expenditures had actually produced any net improvement in the situation of the American people, most reasonable men would have approved them, but there is no evidence that they achieved anything of the sort. On the contrary, all the evidence indicates that they made the situation worse than it was before. We have not only acquired a vast new population of morons; we have inculcated all morons, young or old, with the doctrine that the decent and industrious people of the country are bound to support them for all time.

The effects of that doctrine are bound to be disastrous soon or late. There can be nothing even remotely approaching a rational solution of the fundamental national problems until we face this most important of all of them in a realistic spirit. It would be absurd to look to politicians for leadership here. It is to their interest to build up as large a *bloc* of imbecile partisans as they can rake together. No politician is ever benefited by saving money; it is spending it that makes him.

221

IT IS silly to speak of nuns as burdens on productive workers. They earn their way abundantly, for they get a great deal less for their labor than any women in secular life. Precious few of them give over their whole time to their devotions; the rest are hard at work for long hours every day. If they are worthy of being denounced, it should be as scab competitors, not as parasites.

The better the woman, the more tragic the fate which makes her a nun. It involves the complete destruction of all the qualities which make women amusing and stimulating. The remaining female qualities, to be sure, are accentuated, but probably not enough to compensate for those destroyed. A nun, at best, is only half a woman, just as a priest is only half a man.

222

THERE is great need of a history of political corruption in America. The notion that it was introduced by Jackson is in error, though he undoubtedly greatly prospered it. It actually existed in the earliest colonial days, and in Boston it had reached an elaborate organization by the first years of the Eighteenth Century. There were long periods in the history of most American States when scarcely an honest and capable man was in office. Indeed, there are probably States in which no such man has ever been seen. Yet most American historians treat the politics of the country as a struggle between rival ideas. It actually is, and always has been, a mere struggle between rival gangs of looters and exploiters.

223

WHENEVER one comes to close grips with so-called idealism, as in war time, one is shocked by its rascality.

224

THE POOR fish who used to be robbed by bankers and specu-
lators is now robbed by those who profess to save him. The
bankers always achieved their robbery with the aid of a sort
of psychological sop: they convinced their victim that he
would get rich quickly. The new saviors simply substitute
the delusion that all getting rich is at an end. Neither pretense had any truth in it, but the poor fish is robbed in any
case. The only difference he experiences is a difference in
the anesthetics used to disarm him.

It seems to be an inevitable law of human nature that
the people who produce the wealth of the world should be
deprived of it by those who know how to fool them. When
the workingman escapes the clutches of a rapacious em-
ployer it is usually only to fall into the clutches of a rapacious labor leader or politician. The working people of
Russia are certainly no better off under Communism than
they were under Czarism. All they have gained is a new
delusion, to wit, the delusion that they own Russia. They
own it only in the sense that the prisoners in a house of
correction own the stone walls and steel bars. The product
of their work is vested in their political bosses, and what
they get back of it is only a sort of dole.

I am not aware that there is any remedy for this. There
are inevitable differences in human capacity, and especially
in the capacity for acquiring money. The man in whom it
is highly developed is bound to get more than the man who
has little of it or lacks it altogether. His common method is
not to loot the worker by force, but by cunning. That is to

say, he besets the worker with specious logic, and fills him with disarming delusions. He is then ready to be relieved of his earnings.

225

THE LEGISLATIVE arm is always the most disreputable. The chief executive of the state is at least a picturesque and enviable figure, and the boobs quickly convert the enviable into the heroic. Similarly the judiciary, whatever its defects otherwise, is at least presumed to be intelligent and incorruptible. But no one ever thinks of a legislature as heroic, or as intelligent, or incorruptible. Its internal combats constantly wreck its dignity. Whenever there is a debate in a legislature either one side or the other has to lose, and the one that loses inevitably looks silly. This appearance of silliness gradually extends itself to the whole body, and in the end the legislature is held in contempt.

By the English theory, Parliament is supreme, but everyone knows that public respect for it is very slight. The English plain people reserve their reverence for the king and the judiciary. Theoretically, Parliament is the superior of both, but no Englishman ever thinks of it as such. It appears to him much as Congress appears to an American. Despite the sorry example of Edward VIII, the English go on cherishing all sorts of illusions about the virtue and wisdom of their kings, and even worse illusions about the virtue and wisdom of their courts, but they never show signs of entertaining such illusions about Parliament. They are always ready to criticize it violently. Lloyd George's long warfare with the Lords will be recalled. It was carried on in terms that would have shocked even the most cynical

Englishman if the crown had been the target. In the same way it is rare to find any Englishman criticizing the national courts, though they are in many ways extremely backward, and very far from judicially fair. Even when a given decision is criticized (usually in a very gingerly manner), no question is ever raised about the good faith of the judges involved. But when Parliament is criticized the good faith of its members is questioned openly, and in very offensive terms.

2 2 6

THE FUTILITY of war never occurs to the actual soldier. He pursues his grisly occupation just as any other ignorant man pursues *his*. That he is a victim of quacks never occurs to him until long after the war is over, if then. While he is in the army he looks upon himself with satisfaction and upon his trade with pride. This complaisance is common, of course, to all ignorant men. If they were not so easily deluded the work of the world would never be done. High-toned humanitarians constantly overestimate the sufferings of those they sympathize with. Looking at a man drawing gasoline in a filling-station, they conclude that his life must be dull and miserable. As a matter of fact, he is usually proud of his job, and enjoys his work. This is true of even the most unlikely occupations. I remember well meeting a streetcar conductor in Baltimore who told me that he was saving his money in order to buy a hot-dog stand out Wilkens Avenue where the cars stopped. The Italian who owned it worked sixteen or eighteen hours a day, and probably made only a meagre living, but the car conductor looked upon him with envy. He believed that running such a stand was a pleasant

business, largely, I suppose, because there was no boss giving orders, but also because it offered many opportunities
for quiet snoozing, and other opportunities for meeting
large numbers of the sort of people who seemed interesting
and instructive to such a man.

227

No OTHER religious system has such troubles with the sex
question as Christianity. It is, indeed, the most unhealthy of
religions. The muscular Christian of whom so much is
heard from time to time often turns out on examination to
be a homosexual. The pale green, drugstorish asceticism of
Christianity is largely only a revolt of the *Chandala* against
happiness and naturalness—of the sick against health. Paul
was plainly a pathological case, and the same thing may be
said of many Christian heroes since.

228

THE TENDENCY of man to turn to higher powers in time
of trouble may be only a borrowing from the child's tendency to turn to its mother. It is natural for all human beings up to the age of six or seven to regard their mothers
as omnipotent and omniscient, and it is a sad moment in
every child's life when it discovers that this faith is not
borne out by the facts.

229

THE ENGLISH owe a large segment of their boasted liberties
to two divorces—that of Henry VIII and that of John Milton. An investigation would probably show that many other

of the great boons of mankind have similar lowly origins.
No one has ever really found out how Jesus came to start
His crusade. It was obviously inspired by the example of
John the Baptist, but John's origins are even more mysteri-
ous. It would be interesting and instructive if we could find
out why He took to the bush. A woman may have had some-
thing to do with it, or it may have been suggested by the
Roman police.

2 3 0

THE MARXIAN dialectic is simply a theology. That is to say,
it is a kind of occult hocuspocus, one of the chief characters
of which is that the common people cannot understand it.
Reduced to plain English, it always becomes absurd. In
order to make it impressive the Communist theologians
have to outfit it with a vocabulary of formidable but meaningless words. They maintain it in an extremely clumsy and
buzzfuzzian manner. Reading a treatise on it by one of the
great thinkers of the movement is a really dreadful experience. The argument becomes as windy and fantastic as the
argument for Christian Science.

2 3 1

THE NEGROES, unlike all other oppressed races, never dream
of their homeland. Every proposal that they return to
Africa is opposed by the overwhelming majority of them,
and with the indignation proper to an insult. They are
more free in Brazil and Cuba than they will ever be in the
United States, and in such all-Negro countries as Haiti and
Liberia they should have excellent chances to shine, but it
is rare, indeed, for one of them to migrate. This may be lack

of public spirit, but on the other hand it may be intelligence.
The case of the Jews throws some light upon the subject.
Only the smarter sort of Jews are really well-off in Palestine,
and even so they are not nearly so well-off as the smarter
sort of Jews in New York.

232

THE EFFORT to reconcile science and religion is almost always made, not by theologians, but by scientists unable
to shake off altogether the piety absorbed with their mothers' milk. The theologians, with no such dualism addling
their wits, are smart enough to see that the two things are
implacably and eternally antagonistic, and that any attempt
to thrust them into one bag is bound to result in one swal-
lowing the other. The scientists who undertake this mis-
cegenation always end by succumbing to religion; after a
Millikan has been discoursing five minutes it becomes apparent that he is speaking in the character of a Christian
Sunday-school scholar, not of a scientist. The essence of
science is that it is always willing to abandon a given idea,
however fundamental it may seem to be, for a better one;
the essence of theology is that it holds its truths to be eternal and immutable. To be sure, theology is always yielding
a little to the progress of knowledge, and only a Holy Roller
in the mountains of Tennessee would dare to preach today
what the popes preached in the Thirteenth Century, but
this yielding is always done grudgingly, and thus lingers a
good while behind the event. So far as I am aware even
the most liberal theologian of today still gags at scientific
concepts that were already commonplaces in my schooldays.

Thus such a thing as a truly enlightened Christian is hard to imagine. Either he is enlightened or he is Christian, and the louder he protests that he is the former the more apparent it becomes that he is really the latter. A Catholic priest who devotes himself to seismology or some other such safe science may become a competent technician and hence a useful man, but it is ridiculous to call him a scientist so long as he still believes in the virgin birth, the atonement or transubstantiation. It is, to be sure, possible to imagine any of these dogmas being true, but only at the cost of heaving all science overboard as rubbish. The priest's reasons for believing in them is not only not scientific; it is violently anti-scientific. Here he is exactly on all fours with a believer in fortune-telling, Christian Science or chiropractic.

233

THE ENGLISH know how to make the best of things. Their so-called muddling through is simply skill at dealing with the inevitable. Whenever they confront it they make a frank and usually successful effort to evade it or conceal it. There are probably fewer world-savers in England than in any other country. It has never produced a Tolstoi or a Karl Marx.

234

WORLD WAR II destroyed all the old glory of the American world traveller. Let him mention his tours hereafter and he will be confronted by a war veteran who has been much further and seen much wilder and more astonishing places. All the Marco Polos of the next generation will be drawing pensions.

235

LIBERTY is of small value to the lower third of humanity. They greatly prefer security, which means protection by some class above them. They are always in favor of despots who promise to feed them. The only liberty an inferior man really cherishes is the liberty to quit work, stretch out in the sun, and scratch himself.

236

THE ONLY way a government can provide for jobs for all citizens is by deciding what every man shall do. It would be impossible, no matter how enormous the expenditure of public money, to give every man precisely what he wanted. Three-fourths of all the farm hands would want to be clergymen, schoolteachers or politicians. Thus paternalism inevitably becomes despotism. In undertaking to carry the capital burden of feeding the people, it reaches out for complete control over their activities, and even in the long run over their thoughts. A jobholder is anything but a free man, and a mendicant is free even less. When Harry Hopkins hinted that beneficiaries of the various Roosevelt doles would be expected to vote right, he said nothing more than what everyone already knew. The man who feels that he is under obligations to some demagogue to vote one way and not another is obviously not a free citizen in a free state; he is simply a client in the old Roman sense.

Roosevelt transformed millions of Americans from citizens into clients. The direct effect of this was evil, and the indirect effect was even worse, for all these people were robbed of their self-respect, supposing that they had any to begin with. Whatever their pretensions to the contrary, they knew in their hearts that they were not free agents. Gaining their meagre livelihood in what was essentially an ignominious manner, they became ignominious men. It is such persons who now dominate the politics of the United States. The change has been so gradual that many reflective Americans scarcely notice it. Nevertheless, it will probably wreck the Republic in the long run. It is impossible to imagine a free nation dominated by slaves.

237

THE INFLUENZA epidemic of 1919, though it had an enormous mortality in the United States and was, in fact, the worst epidemic since the Middle Ages, is seldom mentioned, and most Americans have apparently forgotten it. This is not surprising. The human mind always tries to expunge the intolerable from memory, just as it tries to conceal it while current.

238

MOST Americans are now mere machine-tenders: the machine is superior to the man. But no machine has yet been invented to do the work of a college president, a United States Senator, or a movie queen.

239

IT IS never possible for a metaphysician to state his ideas in plain English. Those ideas, with few exceptions, are inherently nonsensical, and he is forced to formulate them in a vague and unintelligble jargon. Of late some of the stars

of the faculty have taken to putting them into mathemati-
cal formulae. They thus become completely incomprehensible to the layman, and gain the additional merit of being
incomprehensible also to most other metaphysicians.

240

WHAT the advocates of world courts and other such phantasms always overlook is the circumstance that the national
courts now in existence do not actually dispense justice at
all, but only law, and that this law is frequently in direct
conflict, not only with what at least one of the two litigants
honestly believes to be his rights, but also with what he believes to be his honor. The normal litigation does not end
with both litigants satisfied. It ends with at least one of
them, and often both of them, as sore as a flogged sophomore, and full of a determination to get even with the judge
at the first chance.

In disputes between man and man this dissatisfaction
is not of serious consequence. The aggrieved party, for all
his bawling, is usually too weak to attempt the revenge he
contemplates; unless he is very rich or has extraordinary
political influence the learned judge can afford to laugh at
him and even to kick him out of the hall of justice. If, being
poor and weak, he ventured to denounce the judge as a
scoundrel in open court or to heave a cuspidor at the jury,
the whole strength of the unbiased masses of men would
be exerted to destroy him, for those unbiased men all believe (so long as they are not litigants themselves) that it
is far better to put up with a great deal of injustice than
to have plaintiff and defendant slanging and bombarding

each other on the public street, to the discomfort of everyone else.

This same notion lies behind the recurrent campaigns
for international courts, but it is unsupported, unluckily,
by the same overwhelming force. In disputes between nations there would be no such colossal disproportion between
the strength of the individual litigant and the strength of
society in general. The case would be rather as if a private
litigant, with the judgment against him, had a fair chance
of getting it reversed by slugging the judge. Nine litigants
out of ten, it must be obvious, would open upon His Honor
instantly. And the tenth would do it the moment he
thought the crowd was with him.

Thus the international police court, if it is ever set
up, will have hard sledding, and the learned justices will
probably have to sit in heavily armored conning-towers,
with plenty of Red Cross nurses in attendance. For what
they will dispense, remember, will be law, not justice. If
they could ladle out actual justice it might be different, for
justice sometimes contents even the loser; his finer feelings
conquer his selfishness. But never law. The mildest man,
when the law bites him, yells for its repeal; the average man
denounces all its agents and catchpolls as scoundrels. Now
imagine these agents and catchpolls the nominees, at least
in part, of his opponent! Imagine it impossible to obtain
absolutely unbiased judges without appointing Hottentots
who can neither read nor write.

2 4 1

THE ONLY guarantee of the Bill of Rights which continues to have any force and effect is the one prohibiting quartering troops on citizens in time of peace. All the rest have been disposed of by judicial interpretation and legislative whittling. Probably the worst thing that has happened in America in my time is the decay of confidence in the courts. No one can be sure any more that in a given case they will uphold the plainest mandate of the Constitution. On the contrary, everyone begins to be more or less convinced in advance that they won't. Judges are chosen not because they know the Constitution and are in favor of it, but precisely because they appear to be against it.

2 4 2

THE SOUTH is one of the few regions in Christendom wherein it is still socially dangerous for a man to express belief in the ordinary principia of science. Northerners who are unfamiliar with the Southern mind are always loath to believe this, but it is a fact. Revivals still go on annually at nearly all of the principal sub-Potomac colleges, and in the smaller ones they are as important in the calendar as the annual football combats. It is impossible to imagine anything properly describable as civilization in a region so dreadfully beset by organized imbecility. If any actual Southerner has ever spoken out openly and bravely against the tyranny of its reigning Protestant shamans I have not heard of him. They all devote themselves to a furious debate over irrelevances, and usually end by putting the blame for all the troubles in the South on a Northern conspiracy. No such conspiracy exists. The North itself would be far better off if the South were more civilized.

243

Is A young man bound to serve his country in war? In addition to his legal duty there is perhaps also a moral duty, but it is very obscure. What is called his country is only its government, and that government consists merely of professional politicians, a parasitical and anti-social class of men. They never sacrifice themselves for their country. They make all wars, but very few of them ever die in one. If it is the duty of a young man to serve his country under all circumstances then it is equally the duty of an enemy young man to serve *his*. Thus we come to a moral contradiction and absurdity, so obvious that even clergymen and editorial writers sometimes notice it.

244

It is folly to argue that the truth of a religion depends upon objective evidence. Christianity might still be true even if the Bible were a proved forgery and the Pope an admitted swindler. The Catholic theologians are smart enough to see this point, and so admit that there have been Popes who were evil characters and are probably in Hell. Religion is simply a cosmology at bottom—a theory of the nature and operations of the universe. It appears in a man simply because man is the only animal, so far as we know, who can ponder on his situation. The idea of immortality is not necessary to religion, but the idea that man is in some way related to higher powers is.

245

THE DEMOCRATIC tendency to make gods of successful politicians makes it all the more necessary to oppose them vigorously. If they were thought of by the public as mere men it might be possible to allow a great deal for their common human fallibility, but once they become gods it is reasonable and just to estimate them as gods. Naturally enough, they all fail miserably by that test. So far as I can recall, I have never written a single commendatory word of any sitting President of the United States. My belief is that the assumptions of the common run of men run so unfairly in his favor that any man who pretends to a reasonable intelligence must necessarily be against him *à outrance*.

246

THE FUNDAMENTAL cause of panics and business depressions is probably nothing more subtle than the desire to get something for nothing. It is probably just as dangerous to push wages too high as it is to overexpand capital. Both devices create fictitious wealth, and when, by the operation of natural laws, its fictitiousness is eventually proved, a collapse follows.

247

MAN HAS to lug around a frame packed with defects, from imperfectly centered eyes to weakly arched feet. He has a poorly arranged spine which imposes too much weight on the fifth lumbar vertebra. He has a miserable arrangement of the gall bladder, which, by lying in him upside down and thus inhibiting the flow of bile, predisposes him to gall-stones. He has a large bowel that requires musculai effort to force its contents up the ascending colon, and then shove them across the transverse colon to the descending one. He has an aorta which, as it leaves the heart, curves off too abruptly and lacks sufficient musculature to endure easily the volume of blood under pressure. He has poorly coated veins with a tendency to varicosis. He has a sagging exposed abdomen with a tendency to hernia.

248

EXPERIENCE is a poor guide to man, and is seldom followed. A man really learns little by it, for it is narrowly limited in range. What does a faithful husband know of women, or a faithful wife of men? The generalizations of such persons are always inaccurate. What really teaches man is not ex-perience, but observation. It is observation that enables him to make use of the vastly greater experience of other men, of men taken in the mass. He learns by noting what hap-pens to them. Confined to what happens to himself, he labors eternally under an insufficiency of data.

249

THE REPORTS of the Judge Advocate General of the Army showed that 75% of all the youths and men conscripted in World War I made some sort of effort to escape service. There are no figures for World War II, but they probably do not differ materially, though their true proportions are concealed somewhat by the fact that fewer avenues of escape offered than in World War I. In brief, conscription in both cases involved the virtual enslavement of multitudes of young Americans who objected to it. But having been forced to succumb, most of them sought to recover their dignity by pretending that they succumbed willingly and even eagerly. Such is the psychology of the war veteran. He goes in under duress, and the harsh usage to which he is subjected invades and injures his ego, but once he is out he begins to think of himself as a patriot and a hero. The veterans of all American wars have resisted stoutly any effort to examine realistically either the circumstances of their service or the body of idea underlying the cause they were forced to serve. Man always seeks to rationalize his necessities—and, whenever possible, to glorify them.

250

ALTRUISM is of dubious character, and the fact that it is a blood relative to self-interest is never quite concealed. Even the sisters in the hospitals do not labor there out of sheer love of humanity: they also hope and believe that they will be rewarded magnificently post-mortem. Christianity probably promotes socially useful actions more than any other major religion, but even Christianity also promotes some that are assuredly not. The solitary Trappist in his cell certainly cannot be described as a useful citizen; on the contrary, he is a burden upon useful citizens. But most Christian ascetics carry on work that is of some ponderable benefit, directly or indirectly, to other persons. This is not true of the ascetics of Brahmanism. They are quite as useless as so many Trappists, and even dirtier. Mohammedanism has little more to show. Most of its major virtues are either useless or anti-social. It teaches its votaries to die complacently in war, which is an indirect benefit to humanity in general though perhaps not to the actual enemy, but otherwise its post-mortem rewards go for such silly things as flattering Allah by rote, making pilgrimages to Mecca, and begetting sons.

251

IT SEEMS to be the general opinion of Americans that all aristocracies, and especially the Prussian aristocracy, are essentially and incurably immoral. In the sense that they are without restraints upon their conduct this idea is plainly absurd: as a matter of fact, the code they recognize and obey is much more severe than that of the common people. But in the sense that they do not accept the code of the common people it is true enough. They show but small respect for the virtue of the common man's wife, and but little more for his own life and property. Worse, they have a taste for war that alarms and revolts him, for when they yield to it it is largely at his expense. They lead him bravely and certainly do not spare themselves, but neither do they spare him. This taste for war is an atavistic relic of an early stage of civilization, and it is thus not illogical to say that aristocracies are barbarous. Industrialism, with its great changes in the organization and ideas of the world, has scarcely touched them. Among other men it has made orderliness and docility capital virtues, but a true aristocracy disdains docility and subscribes only to an orderliness that is all its own. In its relations with common men it does pretty much as it pleases. All of its restraints bear only upon its dealings with its own members.

252

METAPHYSICS is a refuge for men who have a strong desire to appear learned and profound but have nothing worth hearing to say. Their speculations have helped mankind hardly more than those of the astrologers. What we regard as good in metaphysics is really psychology: the rest is only blah. Ordinarily, it does not even produce good phrases, but is dull and witless. The accumulated body of philosophical speculation is hopelessly self-contradictory. It is not a system at all, but simply a quarreling congeries of systems. The thing that makes philosophers respected is not actually their profundity, but simply their obscurity. They translate vague and dubious ideas into high-sounding words, and their dupes assume, as they assume themselves, that the resulting obfuscation is a contribution to knowledge.

253

THE ROTARIANS and their imitators, now almost forgotten, were simply stupid fellows seeking a substitute for the Christianity they could no longer believe in. They had begun to gag at its theology, but could not quite rid themselves of its moral and messianic itches. Thus they set out to abolish war, to gild and cushion the teeth of the profit system, and to bring in a long series of other grandiose reforms, all of them as impossible as squaring the circle. Happily, there was never anything sadistic in this lust for what they called Service: they never advocated clubbing, jugging or hanging the persons who stood aloof from their singing-circle. Thus they differed radically from the theologians whom they sought, perhaps unwittingly, to displace. They always avoided pressure politics, and paid cash out of their own pockets for all their crusades. So carrying on their hocus-pocus, they showed the world that it was possible to invent a moral system that was not a public nuisance—something never before achieved by mankind. They were, to be sure, comic characters, but only in the benign sense that a dog chasing its tail is a comic character. As one who spent a good deal of time and energy, in their heyday, crying them down, I am glad to make this public confession of their innocence. The fundamental and perhaps only real objection to them was that all the things they believed in most earnestly were palpably not true. But that folly was certainly not peculiar to them.

254

WAR STILL shows some of its old glory, but there can be no denying the fact that it tends to deteriorate. The soldiers in the field are chiefly poor conscripts, all of them eager to get home as soon as possible and see to their pensions. The commanders are slaves of political mountebanks and the newspapers, made and broken at the word of bounders. The thing begins to lack all gallantry, all high romance, even all common decency. There is no room in it for an Old Dessauer, a Lafayette, a Prince Eugene. What was once a matter of individual enterprise and valor, a fight between brave men, now tends to become a struggle between machines. Yesterday the danger that a soldier ran in the field was the

danger of a duellist with sword in hand; today it is much
more like the danger of a hog in a slaughter-house.

255

WHATEVER may be the good faith of the plain people in
their recurrent moral rages, it must be obvious that the
politicians who heat them up are mainly frauds. This has
been visible in every war that the United States has ever
seen, including even the Revolution. The more the history
of the revolutionary era is studied, the more it becomes apparent that most of the current prophets were smart fellows
with something to sell. Sam Adams offers an excellent example, and John Hancock is another; there were plenty
more to the southward. Abolition, a moral movement quite
typical of America, was largely staffed by shysters of the
same sort. The example of Prohibition is too recent to need
mention. Its clerical leaders were all fanatics lusting to rule
or ruin, and their political accomplices were almost unanimously plain mountebanks. I was familiar with both groups
during the 1910–30 period, and I can think of no exception. Bishop Cannon was a sadist not far from downright
insanity, and most of the more conspicuous drys in the two
Houses of Congress were notoriously boozers. Once I asked
William H. Anderson, then head of the Anti-Saloon League
in Maryland, how it came about that perhaps a majority of
his supporters in the Maryland Legislature were drunkards.
He replied that they were more truthworthy—at least for his
purposes—than honest drys. The latter, two times out of
three, would have ideas of their own, and it would be difficult to keep them from objecting and rebelling against

orders from headquarters. But the dipsomaniacs could be trusted, for all they thought of was their jobs, which the Anti-Saloon League undertook to guarantee. For the rest, they were free to pursue their villainies unimpeded.

256

DEMOCRACY gives the naturally incompetent and envious man the means of working off his dislike of his betters in a lawful and even virtuous manner. Its moral effect is thus inevitably bad. It puts a premium upon one of the basest passions of mankind, and throws its weight against every rational concept of honor, honesty and common decency.

257

THE HUMAN race shows very little natural inclination toward what are called good works. It always has to be goaded into them by professional do-gooders, most of them palpably frauds. This goading has become a great profession in the United States, and offers an excellent living to multitudes of men who seek to avoid honest labor, and would be half starved if they were forced to resort to it. The proposals they advocate sometimes have a considerable plausibility, at least to unreflecting persons, but the means they employ are nearly always theatrical, dishonest and ruinously costly. The abolition of slavery offers a shining example, and the attempt to saddle Prohibition on the country offers another. Even when genuine reforms are effected by this means they commonly cost at least ten times as much as they are worth.

258

THE IDEA seems to be that science is heartless and inhuman
—that it is willing to serve war because it lacks the great
sanitary stimulus of faith, *i.e.*, of faith in Paul's sense, *i.e.*,
"the substance of things hoped for, the evidence of things
not seen." Well, when has that faith ever refused to serve
war?

259

ROOSEVELT II came near being the purest demagogue recorded in history. Even more than Cato the Censor he devoted himself wholeheartedly to arousing fears and foment-
ing hatreds. His whole politics consisted in attempts to
arouse class against class, people against people. There is no
record, so far as I know, of him ever saying a word in praise
of anyone save obvious frauds. Even when he undertook to
defend this or that group he always did it by preaching
hatred of some other group. His twelve years in office, far
from leaving the American people united, left them cursed
by bitter and irrational animosities, some of which will not
be laid for generations. When he died they had more external enemies than ever before, and all those enemies had
sound reasons for hating them. And inside the country he
had impugned the common honesty of every really decent
man, and set the mob upon him.

260

LIFE on this earth is not only without rational significance,
but also apparently unintentional. The cosmic laws seem
to have been set going for some purpose quite unrelated to

human existence. Man is thus a sort of accidental by-product, as the sparks are an accidental by-product of the horseshoe a blacksmith fashions on his anvil. The sparks are far more brilliant than the horseshoe, but all the same they remain essentially meaningless. They constitute, at best, a disease of the horseshoe—they involve a destruction of its tissue. Perhaps life, in the same way, is a disease of the cosmos.

2 6 1

ANY KIND of handicap save one may be overcome by a resolute spirit—blindness, crippling, poverty. The history of humanity is a history of just such overcomings. But no spirit can ever overcome that handicap of stupidity. The person who believes what is palpably not true is hopeless.

2 6 2

THE IDEA that the sole aim of punishment is to prevent crime is obviously grounded upon the theory that crime can be prevented, which is almost as dubious as the notion that poverty can be prevented. The causes of crime, as a matter of fact, are so completely unknown that no plausible scheme for its prevention is possible. But though it can't be prevented in the sense in which Utopians use the word, it can certainly be prevented in the case of the individual criminal. So long as he is locked up he is harmless to the generality of decent people, and the moment he is executed he becomes harmless forevermore, and is cut off from the propagation of criminal progeny. The English hanged out their criminal class in the Eighteenth Century, and as a result England is the most orderly of all great countries today.

263

EVEN religion is largely grounded on common sense, or, at all events, on what passes as such among theologians. We are asked to believe in Christianity on precisely the same considerations offered for believing in democracy. All the rest of it—revelation, the metaphysics borrowed from the Greeks, and so on—is mere excrescence. The theologians always put heavy stress on what they call natural religion— that is, they argue that belief in their balderdash is made mandatory by common observation and experience, which is to say, by common sense. No known religion depends for its authority on revelation alone, or on philosophy alone. It is always appealing to the evidence of the eyes, ears and nose, and many Christian divines argue quite seriously that Christianity might be proved without any resort to revelation at all. Even revelation itself is often supported by an appeal to common sense. An example is offered by the standard argument in favor of the infallibility of the popes. It is based almost wholly on the contention that Jesus could not conceivably have trusted His church to a hierarchy of frauds. The Twelve Apostles were His appointees, and the line of Popes comes down to us from the Twelve Apostles. This argument is surely not to be sniffed at. It has, indeed, a very considerable plausibility. The one defect in it is that its primary postulate—that Jesus was a god—has no support in the known facts, and seems silly to a rational man.

264

IT IS accepted by biologists that inter-fertility is one of the most reliable signs of consanguinity. It establishes, for example, the close relationship between the dog and the wolf, the buffalo and domestic cattle, the horse and the zebra. So far as I know, no one has undertaken a demonstration of a similar relationship between man and the higher apes. Before World War I reports were afloat that some French biologists were about to make the experiment in West Africa, but nothing was heard of it afterward. Inasmuch as the laws of all civilized countries prohibit sexual relations between men and the lower animals, the scene of the proposed trial was removed to Africa, with a female chimpanzee as one party and a male of some primitive tribe as the other. It would now be possible to make the experiment without running afoul of the police, for artificial insemination has become a widespread practise among human beings. A difficulty lies in the fact that female apes are not very fertile in captivity, but perhaps that might be surmounted. If it turned out that man and the apes were mutually fertile, the last props would be knocked from under the theological doctrine of special creation.

265

IN WHAT passes as the popular mind, words, like the ideas they represent, become formalized, fossilized, and emptied of intelligible significance. This is especially (though surely not exclusively) true in America, where all thinking tends to become cant and all language a sort of meaningless slang

—a mere exchange of what the philologists call counter-words, *i.e.*, worn out rubber-stamps. Thus, the concept "aristocrat" tends to become—and has, in fact, already become—extremely narrowed, and with it the meaning of the word. What it connotes, intrinsically, is simply the "best" type of man—that is, the man whose aspirations are directed to the achievement of what is rare and difficult, and not to the achievement of what is easy and mean—the man, in brief, whose capacities differ positively from those of the average man, not only quantitatively but also qualitatively, and whose activity is spent in doing what the average man is unable to do or afraid to do. But in the United States *aristocrat* has become almost indistinguishable from *loafer*.

266

IN TIME of war, as in time of peace, admiration is lavished upon physical bravery, and the prevailing hero is one who has risked his life for a presumably holy cause. Such men, I confess, leave me cold, for it must be obvious that their merit, such as it is, is very far from uncommon, and I have a considerable doubt that it is really admirable. I can see nothing superior in a man willing to trade his life for public applause, and I can see no more superiority in him when he is a soldier than when he is a prize fighter, a lion tamer, or a parachute-jumper at a county fair. His estimate of his own value is probably more or less accurate, but it is plainly not such as to flatter his parts. The kinds of courage I really admire are not whooped up in war, but cried down, and indeed become infamous. No one, in such times of irrational and animal-like emotion, ever praises the man who

stands out against the official balderdash, and seeks to re-
store the national thinking, so called, to a reasonable sanity.
On the contrary, he is regarded as a shabby and evil fellow,
and there is not much protest when he is punished in a
summary and barbaric manner, without any consideration
whatever of the evidence against him. It is sufficient that he
refuses to sing the hymn currently lined out. That alone is
enough to condemn him.

2 6 7

ONE OF the capital errors of the Founding Fathers was to
discourage the rise of an aristocracy. They were mainly up-
starts themselves, and so disliked men of higher and more
secure status; in fact, the Revolution was largely an uprising
of a class of newly enriched individuals who itched for
honors and offices. Unfortunately, the only superiority they
could think of was that of superior wealth, so they made it
a kind of criterion for the whole country. The result is that
the United States has produced a plentiful plutocracy, but
has never been able to develop a true aristocracy. The so-
called First Families of any American region are seldom
gentry in any rational sense. Their position is founded nine
times out of ten on mere money, and when that is not true
its basis is commonly only political power, a value even
more transitory and meretricious.

The United States is probably the only country ever
heard of on earth in which stockbrokers are almost *ipso
facto* members of good society. Even the Jews among them
acquire a certain enhancement of status. In all other societies that I know of they sit below the salt, and in many

keep his place. The Jew suffers from the same cause, but to a much less extent.

273

THE COMMON argument that crime is caused by poverty is a kind of slander on the poor. Judging by the uplifters' statistics every inhabitant of a slum area should end in the death-house. Actually, the overwhelming majority grow up into respectable citizens, and some of them become citizens of genuine dignity and value.

274

THE THEORY that every avenue of education, up to and including the graduate school, should be thrown open to the poor boy has a virtuous sound, and it may be that there is even a certain amount of sense in it. Obviously, a boy of really high abilities is occasionally born to an indigent family. But this probably happens very seldom, and when it does happen it seems to be due to one of two causes: either a family of proved ability has come, by sheer ill luck, upon extraordinarily rough days, or some female member of an inferior family has submitted her person to a superior stranger. The number of such cases is not large at best— probably not large enough to be significant statistically, and certainly not large enough to justify wasting huge sums of money upon an effort to educate dolts. This last is what is now going on in the United States. The high-schools and State universities swarm with such dolts. Not one in a thousand of them ever returns, in social values, the money laid out upon trying to make him something that he is not.

275

DESPITE all the fine theorizing against it, the Roosevelt type of man must always remain a far more representative symbol of human greatness than the Beethoven type. The reason is not far to seek. The Roosevelt type symbolizes the satisfaction of aspirations that are in practically all men, high and low; the Beethoven type symbolizes aspirations that are in relatively few men. A Roosevelt represents realized power—and all men crave power and the things that go with it. Every man, however humble his lot, sees himself in his secret dreams in situations of power; he thinks of himself constantly as dominating some other man or woman; to the last he never accepts the fact of his own impotence. The Roosevelt type thus represents his ideal. He would enjoy being a Roosevelt vastly more than he would enjoy being a Beethoven. It is thus a waste of words to argue with him that the Roosevelts represent false values, dangerous values, anti-social values. Every man, in his heart, longs to be false, *i.e.*, to be something that he isn't. Every man longs to be powerful. Every man is intrinsically anti-social.

276

THE ESSENTIAL weakness of labor unions, as rational entities, is the essential weakness of democracy as a political system, to wit, that they are run, not by the superior fringe of their members, but by the inferior fringe. There is probably no case in history of a really first-rate workman becoming a successful union politician. Such a politician may have qualities that are not to be sneezed at, but they are not the qualities of a sound craftsman. Nor does he, in his everyday operations, represent the sound craftsmen in his union; he represents predominantly the bunglers and slackers, the malcontents and boss-haters. It is thus no wonder that unions, taking one with another, do next to nothing to improve and safeguard the craftsmanship of their members. Their influence is always thrown in the other direction: that is, they seek to take away from the superior craftsman all his natural advantages, and to reduce him to the level of his inferiors. The tendency is always to make the compensation of the latter precisely equal to that of the former, and to protect dolts and shirkers against the just consequences of their laziness and incompetence. That superior men survive at all under such a system is really remarkable, for they seldom get any comfort out of their superiority. On the contrary, they are frowned upon by the general, and go through life under suspicion. Thus they tend to withdraw from union activities, and to leave the management of affairs to their inferiors, who put into office gabby fellows who know little about the trade they pretend to foster, and care even less. If a given local has two candidates for president before it—one a diligent and skillful master of the craft, and the other a loafer with a loud voice and a high capacity for making promises—it must be obvious that the loafer will get the majority of votes. Very few American unions have ever shown any interest, even the most academic, in promoting the dignity and technic of their crafts. Their sole purpose seems to be to get the highest possible wages and the shortest working hours for the least competent. Their ideal member is apparently a shirker and fumbler who barely qualifies at all. Even their concern about apprentices is seldom, if ever, a concern about the training of really good workmen. What they are really interested in is to keep out as many aspirants as possible, and so increase the market value of the journeyman. Whether or not that journeyman can perform competently the services that he is paid for performing is something that interests them very little.

277

WHEN a democratic government does a wise thing it usually does it for a foolish reason. The collapse of Prohibition in 1932 was probably due in the main to the general belief that abandoning it would bring back prosperity—in fact, it was mainly on that ground that the wet politicians carried on their campaign. Very little was heard during that campaign of the argument that Prohibition was essentially tyrannical and infamous. All the politicoes were afraid to raise the point. They confined themselves to the contention that resuming brewing and distilling would make farmers rich. What they really had their eyes on, of course, was the revenue from excises and licenses. That revenue has been enormous, and every cent of it has been spent on new schemes for rounding up the votes of imbeciles.

278

MAN SHARES his indomitability with all the other creatures, but his capacity for hope is said to be his alone. In its essence, of course, it is only a phase of his singular capacity for believing the obviously not true. Not one man in a million ever actually sees his dreams realized. The portion of all the rest is disappointment and disillusionment. Human life is thus a sort of massive irrationality. The idea that chiefly animates it, and in a sense glorifies it, is an idea whose falsity is made manifest by all experience. Man spends his days in the manner of a rabbit trying to fly, or a wren striving to lay an egg as big as an ostrich's.

But is his capacity for hope really peculiar to him? I suspect that the common assumption that it is may be blown up as our knowledge of the lesser creatures widens. Is the ant, say, or the bee a mere automaton? Isn't it harder to believe that he is than to believe that he, too, has his visions and his aspirations? Certainly an ant spends a great deal of his time in carrying on enterprises that never come off. Some of them are relatively complicated, and in order to project them he must have something properly describable as a conception of them, a picture in his mind of what they will or may lead to. When they fail, he must be disappointed, and if he is capable of disappointment he is also capable of hope. Here is a field in which little really informing work has been done. There has been some investigations, of course, of the psychology of the lower animals, even of the amoebae. But all such investigations have been hobbled and colored by *à priori* notions that no creature below the rank of man can formulate a genuine idea. I doubt it.

279

G. K. CHESTERTON was a smart fellow, and wrote very effectively. To be sure, his method was monotonous, for four-fifths of his essays start off by citing something that is generally believed, and then seek to demolish it by the devices of casuistry. But he was actually a very clever casuist, and so his performance is often amusing. His defect lay in the fact that the ideas he chose to demolish were often more or less true, and that those he set up in place of them were nearly always plain nonsense. A reader who really follows him starts out in the Nineteenth Century and lands in the Thirteenth.

280

THE SQUALOR of war is seldom complained of by soldiers. In all healthy men there seems to be an unquenchable boyish liking for going dirty. This explains the popularity of camping-out. I have myself no taste for camping-out, for it involves hard physical work and also participation in sports, *e.g.*, fishing, that bore me. But when I know that I am to be home all day Sunday, with no visitors, I never shave, and it delights me to get into old shoes and overalls, and make myself filthy pottering in the backyard. My old taste for bricklaying was probably mainly a taste for doing something dirty. Soldiers returning from the wars never complain of the cooties; they boast of them.

281

DEMOCRACY always tends toward an unhealthy exaltation of incompetence. The abject and useless man becomes a sort of hero, and the idea that he deserves to get whatever he wants leads to the idiotic theory that his deprivations are due to the evil machinations of someone else. It is not enough to be just to him—he must be grossly favored. There is, of course, no genuine justice in any scheme of feeding and coddling a loafer whose only ponderable energies are devoted to reproduction. Nine-tenths of the rights he bellows for are really privileges, and he does nothing whatsoever to deserve them.

282

COMMUNISM, like any other revealed religion, is largely made up of prophecies. When they fail to come off its clergy simply say that they will be realized later on. Thus, if we have another boom, they will argue that the collapse of capitalism is only postponed. The fact that the greatest booms ever heard of followed Marx's formal prophecy of the downfall of capitalism is already forgotten, just as millions have long since forgotten the early Christian prophecy that the end of the world was at hand. The first Christians accepted postponements as docilely as the Communists of today—in fact, many of them were still believing and hoping two hundred years after the crucifixion. In all probability, Communism will last quite as long. It is still in its first century, and so hope still hops high.

283

ALL THE reforms so loudly whooped up involve an effort to change human nature by forcing men and women to do things they don't want to do. It is a vain enterprise. A sea lion remains indubitably a sea lion, even after it has been clubbed and cajoled into balancing a ball on its nose and blowing a cornet.

284

THE PERSONAL austerity of the Puritans was not unique and not new. The Catholic pietists had long surpassed it, both in pretension and in performance. What was novel in it was simply the extraordinary ferocity of its effort to force an uncomfortable way of life upon the other fellow. Puritanism, like democracy, seldom got far from hatred of whoever was having a better time. He was not only a sinner doomed to hell; he was also a private enemy to be smitten on this earth. The same motive is constantly cropping up in democracy. It is, at its best, only a scheme to counteract the natural differences between man and man by setting up artificial likenesses. At its worst, it is a relentless hatred of every sort of superiority. Superiority in wealth is the variety that a democrat hates most, for it offers the advantages that he most esteems and envies, but he is also against all other varieties. The bitter Puritan animosity to Catholic monasticism probably had one of its chief springs in a sneaking fear that monks and nuns, on the awful Day of Judgment, would stand a bit higher at the bar than any money-grubbing, meat-eating and concupiscent Puritan, however prayerful. The recurrent effort to prove that the Puritans were the pioneers of democracy, though based on false premises and animated by dubious motives, nevertheless has some sense in it. They were actually the pioneers of everything that is worst in democracy, including especially hatred of the fellow having a better time. For the good that is (or may) be in it, to wit, the limitation of government, equality before the law, and free speech and conscience, they certainly had no liking. All these things were introduced into the American scheme of things by men who were atheists by the Puritan definition, though they borrowed from Holy Church quite as often as they borrowed from the French

rationalists. It must be obvious that the American scheme
of things no longer includes such concepts. They have been
purged mainly under the influence of the decadent Puritanism that still afflicts the country. Prohibition, to take one
example, was not merely a transient aberration, an accidental and in some sense pathological department from the
true faith of democracy, as we are asked to believe. It was
perfectly characteristic of the Puritanism that has always
been the bedfellow of American democracy. Its malignant
swinishness fitted into the Puritan pattern perfectly.

285

THE ONLY department of so-called philosophy that shows
any general utility is epistemology—the study of the nature
of knowledge, and the means of attaining it. All the rest is
mere logic-chopping, and as lacking in genuine significance
as a series of college yells. It would no doubt surprise the
average man, even the average intelligent man, to learn
that he harbors an epistemology, but such is the fact. In
all men save those poisoned by metaphysical toxins it is the
epistemology of common sense—a product, not of professional philosophers, but of a line of enlightened, practical
men stretching back to the beginnings of the race. The
chief aim of all professional philosophers, now as in the
past, is to break down this admirable epistemology and substitute something more mystical. They are failing as their
predecessors failed—as even another Plato would fail if he
came into the world today. Science in all its ramifications
has no truck with them. They are intellectual acrobats and
sword-swallowers, and of no more practical value to human-

ity than those in the circus. Indeed, they are of less value, for the circus brethren are at least amusing.

2 8 6

THE PREVALENCE of corruption under democracy is probably due, at least in part, to the fact that in a democratic society it never really pays to be honorable. No one believes in honor, and there is no *noblesse oblige*. The prevailing moral system always reduces itself to a craven fear of being caught.

2 8 7

BY AN inferior man I mean one who knows nothing that is not known to every adult, who can do nothing that could not be learned by anyone in a few weeks, and who meanly admires mean things.

2 8 8

PEOPLE crave certainties in this world, and are hostile to ifs and buts. The chief strength of organized religion lies in the fact that it provides plain and positive assurance for poor souls who find the mysteries of this earthly existence an intolerable headache, and are uneasy about their prospects post-mortem. In the political field the same appetite for surety is visible, which explains, of course, the prosperity of demagogues. They are simply persons who promise in loud, ringing voices to solve the insoluble and unscrew the inscrutable. At their worst they are palpable frauds, comparable to so many thimble-riggers at a county fair; at their best they come close to the elegant imbecility of theologians.

289

EVEN in the midst of this peerless democracy, the vote is still called the franchise. It is impossible to distort *franchise* into *right*. It was regarded by the Fathers as a privilege, and they laid elaborate plans to withdraw it whenever its exercise was abused.

290

THE MOST valuable products of war are not material but psychical, and the greatest of them all is the capacity to accept its risks and horrors undismayed, and even a bit gaily and eagerly—in brief, with something approaching delight— in brief, in the militarist spirit. This spirit is native to healthy men. One finds it almost invariably in boys: that is why they make better soldiers than their elders. It is combatted in civilization by that vast complex of moral delusions which wars upon all honest and natural impulses. It is set free, with fine irony, by pitting those delusions against one another. Thus the non-militarist, *i.e.*, the moralist, the "good" man, forces himself into the immorality of war by convincing himself that it is a moral necessity.

Nothing could be more ridiculous. War is never moral, within any intelligible meaning of the term. It is essentially *im*moral; it is, indeed, the master immorality. What men get out of it is a general loosing of the moral straps. It brings out, not what is "best" in them, but precisely what is "worst"—that is, all the savage instincts which morality condemns to the sub-cellar. It enables them to live for a time in unqualified obedience to their natural impulses, *e.g.*, to wound, ravage and destroy. Even the discipline it enforces, though superficially harsh, is actually loose, primitive and in accord with natural desires: one finds wolves, ants and fishes content under it. Its underlying principle is wholly egoistic. Whatever hurts the pack hurts the individual, and hence is immoral, but exactly the same act, launched against the enemy pack, is perfectly moral. Here we have a frank repudiation of the doctrine that acts are moral or immoral in themselves, and a return to the hedonistic opportunism that is native to man.

To wage a war for a purely moral reason is as absurd as to ravish a woman for a purely moral reason. Such notions do not make for innocence, and hence for self-respect; they make for hypocrisy. The more war has to be explained and justified, the less good will issue from it. Nevertheless, even a war corrupted by moral rabbinism is of some benefit to a nation, and particularly to the lower orders thereof. That benefit is analogous to the one that would be conferred upon a pious deacon by a week's drunk, or to the one that an old maid would gain by being dragged to bed by a college sophomore. It sets free the instincts that convention wars upon, and destroys some of the evil fruits of chronic repression.

291

The following was written in 1931, as part of an article for the Baltimore *Evening Sun* that was never printed:

FOR A number of years past the American people have been swooning in a purple light, listening to the sweet, voluptuous music of harps and psalteries. All sorts of quacks have operated upon them, tickling them under the gills, blowing perfumed smoke into their ears, and dancing gaudy jumping-jacks in front of them. Any fraud with an oily tongue and a hopeful air could get a hearing. They hearkened to politicians who told them that all the ancient laws of economics had been repealed, to metaphysicians who proved that a dollar was made up of 200 or 300 cents, and to theologians who assured them *ex cathedra* that they were God's Chosen People, who could not come to grief. The Golden Age, it appeared, had dawned.

In all this there was little save what Al Smith called balony, but it was hard to convince any true American of the fact. I remember well when certain cynical bankers began to hint that stocks selling on a 2% basis were not good buys: their reward was to be accused of trying to start a bear movement and grab the stocks for themselves. Car conductors and police sergeants pulled their money out of the building associations, and put it into securities yielding half as much as a savings account. In Washington, Dr. Hoover flapped his glistening wings, moving majestically toward the White House. Arthur Brisbane warned against selling America short. The radio belched optimism. Europe, one heard, was dying of envy. We were actually inhabiting the New Jerusalem, with walls of alabaster and pavements of gold.

What became of all the cynics in those days I don't know: probably they were hiding in cellars. One heard from them only rarely, and no one would listen to them. But when the blow-off came their prognostications were borne out to the letter. Out of the purple haze emerged a file of dark green facts, and at once it appeared that they were precisely of the cut and nature envisioned by the cynics aforetime. The laws of economics, it turned out, were still in full blast. The contents of a dollar stopped at 100 cents. And God had forgotten His new Chosen People as completely and disastrously as He forgot His old ones in A.D. 70.

292

ONE OF the main differences between the rich and the poor is that the poor accumulate no permanent values, no deposit of durables. The average two-story workingman's house, in Baltimore, begins to fall in even before it is paid for, and there remains of it nothing save a debt. The great accumulations of civilization, whether physical or spiritual, have always been made by a relatively small class. They represent the surplus values that Socialists and other such quacks are always talking of. The workingman accumulates little save useless things, and a year after his death his whole stock is dissipated. He acquires nothing that has any permanent worth.

293

"I will govern according to the common weal, but not according to the common will." James I of England, 1621.

THIS was a rational saying. What reason have we got to believe that the common will works to the common weal? The masses of the people are quite as incapable of deciding questions of government as they are of deciding questions of medicine. In one case as in the other, their decisions are arrived at, not by making an enlightened examination of the facts, but by listening to quacks. There are quacks enough in medicine, God knows, but in politics there is nothing else. This fact is what sets the political trade off from all others. No professional politician can be quite honest, either with himself or with others. However lofty his intentions, he must get into office by abasing himself. Either he must knuckle down to the bosses, or he must court the mob. No other man confronts so hard a choice. It is still possible for a medical man, or even a lawyer, to be completely honorable and yet to make a relatively decent living, but it is virtually impossible for a politician. The minute he makes a serious effort in that direction he loses office, and thus ceases to be a going concern.

294

THE WORST objection to war is not that the fighting injures the bodies of human beings, but that the accompanying hooey pollutes and deteriorates their minds. This is especially true in democratic countries, where demagogy is engaged in a constant effort to that end, even in times of peace. The moment the bugles begin to blow all the worst fools and frauds are turned loose upon the populace, with open license to go as far as they please. The whole power of the state, in fact, is put at their disposal, to protect and foster them in their imbecilities. What they can accomplish, even in a short space, was dreadfully demonstrated in this great Republic during World War I. The American people came out of that heroic combat with very little material damage, but they were so horribly debauched in mind that it took them the better part of a generation to recover. Prohibition was as plainly a result of their addlement as Ku Kluxery.

295

RAY SPRINGLE, a Pittsburgh reporter who went into the South disguised as a Negro and printed his observations in a syndicate of newspapers, laid stress in one of his articles on the difficulties which confront a colored child when it discovers the sharp difference between the two races. This has been noted before, and the same difficulty, though it may be less poignant, confronts a white child who has been brought up with and played with colored children, and then finds one day that they are not her kind. My wife, in fact, based one of her short stories on the latter situation.

I suspect that something of the same dismay must overcome a white child who discovers that its elders are of the submerged class and not regarded with respect by their betters. This discovery, of course, is commonly made gradually, but it must be marked by shocking episodes. I often look at the Oakie children who swarm in West Baltimore since the war, and wonder if they know how low-down their parents are. Some of them, perhaps, never come to realize it, but others undoubtedly do. In school they meet children whose fathers and mothers are palpably superior, and those other children, with the cruelty of childhood, do not hesitate to rub in the fact. It must be dreadfully disconcerting when it is driven home.

296

DEMOCRACY, like virtue, seems to be something that everybody whoops up but nobody follows as a career. Very few Americans actually believe in it. Whenever the test comes they are ready to deprive other people of their rights, and meanwhile they are always willing to exchange their own for some form of security. Their apparent ideal in government is a paternalism that would be as completely unlike democracy as either Communism or Fascism. The number of actual democrats in the United States is always very small, if indeed any such faction ever exists at all. Nine Americans out of ten, when they take an active hand in public affairs, make some effort to destroy one or another of the immemorial democratic principles. This is especially true of the so-called Liberals.

297

IT IS probably true that the advance of civilization will gradually diminish the popularity of war, but it remains doubtful that it will abolish war altogether. The Greeks, by all the standards held up by schoolmasters, were certainly civilized, and yet they fought many wars. The popes, including even some of the best popes, fought even more. Socrates, I believe, boasted of the fact that he had once served in one of the Greek wars. Even today men of no little dignity occasionally make the same boast. The truth is that war remains almost universally popular, as I have argued for years. Every time I do so I am denounced by sentimentalists, but I believe that my case remains a good one. It always takes two or three years of war, with a series of costly disasters, to set up any genuine demand for peace.

298

WHY ASSUME so glibly that the God who presumably created the universe is still running it? It is certainly perfectly conceivable that He may have finished it and then turned it over to lesser gods to operate. In the same way many human institutions are turned over to grossly inferior men. This is true, for example, of most universities, and of all great newspapers.

299

THE MEN who run governments are so incompetent that when by any chance they form a reasonably good one it is a sort of marvel, and makes historians crow and flap their wings—for example, the case of the Founding Fathers. In the ordinary business of the world more efficient structures are erected every day, and without comment—for example, the Great Atlantic & Pacific Tea Company and the Pennsylvania Railroad. Even government, when it hires reasonably competent men for a definite job, sometimes does it well—for example, the Panama Canal.

300

THE TIME must come inevitably when mankind shall surmount the imbecility of religion, as it has surmounted the imbecility of religion's ally, magic. It is impossible to imagine this world being really civilized so long as so much nonsense survives. In even its highest forms religion embraces concepts that run counter to all common sense. It can be defended only by making assumptions and adopting rules of logic that are never heard of in any other field of human thinking.

301

DESPITE all the current blah about new incentives to industry (Communism), the duty of every man to submerge himself in the state (Fascism), and the wickedness of people who save their money and look out for themselves otherwise (the New Deal), individualism still survives in the world, and it will survive until the end of time. Every reflective man knows that even the most elemental sort of co-operation quickly reaches its limit—that all the really important business of the world must be done by single men, operating under compulsion of their own egos. The philosophical attack upon individualism is carried on, quite clearly, by failures. "Individualism is bad for me, Irving Ginsberg; *ergo*, it is immoral and against God." If we are ever to be led out of the present chaos it will be by men no more altruistic than Napoleon I. They will fight their own way out, and take the rest of us with them. This, in brief, is the history of all human progress. An artist does not work for humanity; he works for himself. So does a scientist. So does a financier. So, above all, does a so-called statesman.

There are, of course, persons who are naturally communists, but they are very few. Holy Church, always wise, recognizes that they constitute a separate caste, and so it puts them in monasteries. It is well aware, and says so openly, that they are abnormal. Even Christ spoke of them as eunuchs. If all people were of their sort the world would come to a standstill, as it came near doing in the Ages of Faith. Man holds his lead over woman, as every psychologist knows, because of his greater variability. This variability, at its best, is what we call individualism. The assertive individual is a superior man. He may be highly dangerous at times, but he is nevertheless necessary. In fact, he is the whole human race. The rest are mere ciphers. As Nietzsche said, they may be handed over to statistics and the Devil.

302

IN THE common assumption that the United States received a severe setback when the free land of the West was exhausted there is probably a considerable amount of hooey. The fact is that the settlement of the West made jobs for more men than were ever needed for its actual opening. What is more, they became diverse in character, and so offered attractions to many different kinds of men, some of them superior. The actual pioneers were nearly all third-raters from the exhausted farms and decaying towns of the Eastern seaboard. First-rate men took no part in the movement. It was not until settlements began to grow up that any of them flocked in. This was clearly the case of Oklahoma. The farmers who took part in the land rushes were mainly poor idiots, but some of the schemers and swindlers who followed them were really smart. In all probability, the opportunities in the West for a bright young man are better today than they were in the days when the region was being opened. At that time he had little choice of enterprises; about the only thing he could do was to wear himself out on a prairie farm. But today the opportunities before him are almost as various as they are in the Eastern Gomorrahs.

The influence of F. J. Turner's writings upon the frontier has probably been for the bad. They have been accepted too literally by a whole generation of third-rate historians. The really good historians have always been more or less suspicious of them. Indeed, Turner himself never took them as seriously as most of his followers.

3 0 3

THE IDEA that customs barriers are necessary in order to protect weak and incompetent nations against strong ones is probably false. It is disproved by American experience, and it was disproved by the German Zollverein. The difference between Massachusetts and Mississippi is at least as great as that between England or Germany and Albania, yet Mississippi not only doesn't lose by free trade with Massachusetts; it gains. The divisions between nations are not natural, and the common people seldom of their own motion cherish national animosities. They are promoted by professional politicians, the eternal enemies of human peace and security. It is always to the interest of such politicians to arouse fears. They make their living doing so, and then promising to get rid of the bugaboo by quack devices. One of the worst of these quack devices is the customs barrier. It may have some use in the early days of a rapidly developing nation, but as between nations that have pretty well reached their growth, it is an intolerable evil. What is universally good should be obtainable anywhere, and at substantially the same price. Europe would certainly be better off if the American five-cent cigar of the pre-war years were on sale in all its tobacco shops.

3 0 4

THERE was a great deal of silly talk during World War II about the lack of freedom in the totalitarian countries of

Europe. How much freedom does a man have in rural Arkansas? Certainly it must be very little. He is not only at the mercy of his neighbors' opinions; he is under a constant espionage by the rustic clergy. The truth is that very few human beings really esteem or crave freedom: they are always willing to submit to authority. What happened in Italy and Germany might very well happen in the United States, and without producing any uproar save from a few fanatics. I'd holler myself, but how many other Baltimoreans would? Americans submitted to the atrocities of Prohibition with enormous docility, and during the first few years the overwhelming majority of them made no resistance whatever. Even among the so-called intellectuals there was a strong tendency to submit. Both the *Nation* and the *New Republic* discussed Prohibition as if it were a settled matter. It was only a few fanatics who fought it, and it took them thirteen years to get sufficient support to beat it. In many ways Prohibition was more oppressive than anything ever seen in the totalitarian countries, or even in Russia. It entered the citizen's very home, and completely destroyed his self-respect. Nevertheless, Americans endured it for years, and they'd be enduring it still if it had not been for the hard labor of a very small group of rebels.

305

IT IS not materialism that is the chief curse of the world, as pastors teach, but idealism. Men get into trouble by taking their visions and hallucinations too seriously. The lowly hind, pausing in the furrow to mop his brow, dreams a dream of high achievement in the adjacent city. Ten years later there is a plow standing idle—and another victim of capitalistic tyranny is laboring as a bus conductor.

306

THE QUESTION of the unemployable man has never been dealt with realistically. All the uplifters seek to prove that his incapacity is thrust upon him from without, but in reality it lies within him, and nothing can be done to rid him of it. Even at the peaks of prosperity, whether real or false, many hundreds of thousands of men are quite unable to earn their livings. They may be given seats in the boat, but they are congenitally unable to pull their weight. This sorry class includes all the multitudes of incompetent craftsmen—a large and ever-increasing horde in the United States. There are plumbers in practise who not only do not earn what they demand (and get) for working, but actually do a lot of damage. Their value to society, if it were expressed honestly, would thus be expressed in minus figures, like the value of a theologian, a high-jacker, or the average members of Congress. What is to be done with such men is a problem that the uplifters have failed to solve. Many of them, I suppose, might conceivably earn their sustenance, clothes and housing in less pretentious occupations, and some actually make the descent, but the majority are sustained in their fraud by labor unions and public tolerance. The irrational American confidence in education tends to lift vast numbers of men above their natural levels, and so makes frauds of them. A man who might have made a good carpenter becomes a lawyer, and the man who should have been driving a wagon becomes a carpenter, spoiling good wood, wasting nails and building bad houses. Maybe we need a general reduction in rank of all men. This is the only sort of adjustment in the living standard that has any rationality. But the American people, thanks to the schoolma'am and the political demagogue, have embraced the absurd and dangerous doctrine that every man deserves not only a good job, but also promotion.

307

THE MARXIAN view that all men are money-grubbers and that if let alone they would yield themselves utterly to the profit motive is one more proof that Marxians are money-grubbers themselves. They constitute in the main a class of unsuccessful and envious men, eager for money but unable to get it. Every one of them has his eye on some luckier man who has done what he (the Marxian) tried to do and failed. Inasmuch as the kind of success that the Marxian most envies is in the economic field, his whole philosophy overaccentuates the economic motive. He simply can't imagine a man having any other. As a matter of fact, relatively little of the serious work of the world is done by men moved by the desire for money. The lower down we get the more it is apparent; the higher we go the more it is displaced by other motives. The Marxian thus lives in a world pitched at a very low level. He not only makes his principal appeal to incompetent and useless men; he also falls inevitably into the assumption that the ideas of such men are the ideas of all men.

308

THE PSYCHOLOGISTS and metaphysicians wrangle endlessly over the nature of the thinking process in man, but no matter how violently they differ otherwise they all agree that it has little to do with logic and is not much conditioned by overt facts.

309

THE CHIEF contribution of Protestantism to human thought is its massive proof that God is a bore.

310

WHAT we confront is not the failure of capitalism, but simply the failure of democracy. Capitalism has really been responsible for all the progress of the modern age. Better than any other system ever devised, it provides leisure for large numbers of superior men, and so fosters the arts and sciences. No other system ever heard of is so beneficial to invention. Its fundamental desire for gain may be far from glorious *per se*, but it at least furthers improvement in all the departments of life. We owe to it every innovation that makes life secure and comfortable.

Unfortunately, like any other human institution (for example, Holy Church), capitalism tends to run amuck when it is not restrained, and democracy provides inadequate means of keeping it in order. There is never any surety that democracy will throw up leaders competent to discern the true dangers of capitalism and able to remedy them in a prudent and rational manner. Thus we have vacillated between letting it run wild and trying to ruin it. Both courses are hazardous and ineffective, and it is hard to say which is the more so.

311

THE CHRISTIAN church, in its attitude toward science, shows the mind of a more or less enlightened man of the Thirteenth Century. It no longer believes that the earth is flat, but it is still convinced that prayer can cure after medicine fails.

312

LINCOLN'S saying in his Peoria speech of October 16, 1854, that "No man is good enough to govern another man without that other's consent" sounds virtuous, but it is actually nonsense. Nearly half the American people at any given time have refused their consent to the current government. To be sure, they have to endure it, but that is something quite different from consenting to it. The plain fact is that government is always an imposition. It represents in the last analysis a conquest, and when that conquest is made with ballots they are no more than surrogates for bullets, for as someone has truly said, voting is simply a way of determining which side is the stronger without putting it to the test of fighting. Only the stupid submit to defeat at the polls with complete resignation. All even half-intelligent persons, when the other side wins, lay plans at once for either vitiating the victory or changing it into defeat at some future time.

313

THE RELATION of the brain weight to the total body weight in man is as one is to 36. But in the rat it is as one is to 28 and in the canary-bird as one is to 12.

314

UNDER the American system of government it is very hard to get rid of an incompetent or dishonest man in a high place. The process of impeachment is cumbersome and uncertain, and political skulduggery always impedes it. Moreover, it does not provide any punishment for the dolt or knave impeached, save only removal from office. The English got rid of Edward VIII much more facilely than the United States can get rid of a corrupt judge or congressman.

315

THE RUSSIAN constitution, adopted on December 5, 1936, reads as if it were written by Thomas Jefferson. In fact, large parts of it *were* written by Jefferson—and smouched by Stalin. Other parts were borrowed from Lincoln, Tennyson and Edgar Guest. But it has no more relation to actual events in Russia than the Democratic platform of 1932 had to the course of the New Deal.

316

IN THE long run it will most likely turn out that planning economies is as hopeless as planning the weather. In both cases the most we can do is to develop forecasting into a more or less exact science. Even so, it will be impossible to forecast the psychological reactions of the people, though those reactions must enter into every planned economy that is rational at all. Thus the whole planning business is upset by unknown and dubious factors.

3 1 7

THE MILITARY caste did not originate as a party of patriots, but as a party of bandits. The primeval bandit chiefs eventually became kings. Something of the bandit character still attaches to the military professional. He may fight bravely and unselfishly, but so do gamecocks. He may seek no material rewards, but neither do hunting dogs. His general attitude of mind is stupid and anti-social. It was a sound instinct in the Founding Fathers that made them subordinate the military establishment to the civil power. To be sure, the civil power consists largely of political scoundrels, but they at least differ in outlook and purpose from the military, and to some extent at least, they are superior. A country dominated by the military is always backward, and frequently almost savage. Even Frederick the Great, perhaps the most successful military king in modern history, always tried to make it plain that he was first a civilian and only secondarily a military leader. He never allowed his military chiefs anything resembling civil power. As for himself, he always argued that he was not the commander of the state, but its first servant. Nine-tenths of his energies were devoted, not to military enterprises, but to civil reforms. He was primarily a first-rate administrator, and he took to war only in defense of his administration.

3 1 8

THE STATE is not force alone. It depends upon the credulity of man quite as much as upon his docility. Its aim is not merely to make him obey, but also to make him want to obey.

319

UNQUESTIONABLY, the congenitally unlucky man deserves sympathy, but equally unquestionably that sympathy in the long run can never take the form of handing over to him the goods of the lucky. Their superiority, in that one respect at least, will remain unchanged, and they will go on benefiting from it.

320

WHAT Nietzsche meant by a good war was one waged gallantly, daringly, above all, *not* morally. No such good war is imaginable to a democratic people.

321

DESPITE ten thousand New Deals, nothing whatever can be done in the long run for the man who is stupid and lazy, and has more children than he can care for. He not only engenders a great deal of misery in his own family; he also tends to destroy the happiness of his neighbors. He is, indeed, a wretchedly bad neighbor, as he is a bad citizen. His imbecility puts a heavy burden on better men, and exposes them and their families with them to a long series of hazards that they should not be asked to face. Any man, having a child or children he can't support, who proceeds to have another should be sterilized at once. It makes no difference whether his misfortunes are due to his own inferiority or to mere bad luck. Whatever their cause, he has no right to produce another poor fish to share them. Certainly even the most violent supporters of the doctrine that there is good blood in the proletariat must admit that it is socially dangerous to bring up children in starving households. The effect upon even a talented child of living on charity throughout its youth is inevitably disastrous. It will grow up cherishing the unsound and anti-social theory that its neighbors owe it a living.

3 2 2

A LARGE part of the democratic objection to new forms of government reads precisely like Metternich's objection to democracy. We must grasp the idea that democracy is really not final and absolute, and that totalitarianism in some form or other may succeed it. Roosevelt II's frequent insistence that there is something good in mere experiment may have the effect in the long run of paving the way for a genuinely revolutionary novelty. O. W. Holmes, Felix Frankfurter and other such advocates of trial and error in government headed the same way. Soon or late one is bound to come along with the notion that *no* form of democracy is feasible—that is, that we must strike out into new fields. Inasmuch as man is always intensely imitative, we'll strike out inevitably into fields already explored by others. Totalitarianism violates a number of ancient American prejudices, but there is certainly no ground in history for assuming that those prejudices are ineradicable. Men have changed their basic ideas very frequently in the past, and they may do so hereafter. We have abandoned the restraints of the Constitution, and set ourselves on the road to novelty.

3 2 3

THE KIND of man who wants the government to adopt and enforce his ideas is always the kind of man whose ideas are idiotic.

3 2 4

THERE is a good deal of confusion between the objects of religion and its devices. The ceremonials of all sects, as they accumulate formalism, lose their original significance, and begin to pick up concretions from extraneous emotions. Not a few of them, for example, show an unmistakable sexual element, and all of them tend to be colored by poetry. But at the bottom of every one of them is the primary religious impulse—to propitiate superhuman powers that are supposed to take a hand in the affairs of man. Take that away, and what remains is not religion at all.

3 2 5

THE PITTSBURGH STOGIE, in my early days, was made of American tobacco and tended to be coarse in flavor, but it had one great superiority over the cheap cigars of the time: it was hand-rolled and hence free drawing. The smoker seldom encountered a stogie that was what the trade calls a plug. But with changes in the manufacturing process plugs have become common, and in 1944 I got a box in which at least half of the contents were unsmokable without cutting back an inch or more from the twist. Perhaps it was only a coincidence that this box was marked "Union Made."

326

A GOVERNMENT can never be the impersonal thing described in textbooks. It is simply a group of men like any other. In every 100 of the men composing it there are two who are honest and intelligent, ten obvious scoundrels and 88 poor fish.

327

THE WORST government is the most moral. One composed of cynics is often very tolerant and humane. But when fanatics are on top there is no limit to oppression.

328

SINCE the year 476 the history of Italy has been one long chronicle of dishonor. Down to 1860 the country was almost constantly under foreign rule, and all its local governments were grounded upon oppression tempered by assassination. In World War I it ratted on its allies, and in World War II it ratted again. Such is the heir and assign of the Rome of Caesar and Augustus!

329

MY OLD suggestion that public offices be filled by drawing lots, as a jury box is filled, was probably more intelligent than I suspected. It has been criticized on the ground that selecting a man at random would probably produce some extremely bad State governors. I am not so sure of it, but even if the objection is sound it could be met by setting up a sort of panel for the higher public offices—a panel confined to men who had in some way or other proved their capacity for managing relatively large affairs. I think I'd exclude all lawyers and journalists at the start, and obviously it would be wise to exclude all men who had been convicted of crime, or even plausibly accused of it. There also might be age limits, both upper and lower, and qualifications regarding property and residence. But I incline to believe that it would be best to choose members of the Legislature quite at random. No matter how stupid they were, they could not be more stupid than the average legislator under the present system. Certainly they'd be measurably more honest, taking one with another. Finally, there would be the great advantage that all of them had got their jobs unwillingly, and were eager, not to spin out their sessions endlessly, but to get home as soon as possible.

330

UNDER democracy one party always devotes its chief energies to trying to prove that the other party is unfit to rule—and both commonly succeed, and are right. The Coolidge Prosperity and the Hoover Economy of Plenty were quite as bad as the New Deal. The United States has never developed an aristocracy really disinterested or an intelligentsia really intelligent. Its history is simply a record of vacillations between two gangs of frauds.

331

THE EARLY Christians believed in the imminent end of the world mainly because they were hard up, and suffering all sorts of pains and inconveniences. The fact that there were happy people in the world apparently never occurred to them. When they heard happiness mentioned they always put it down to sin.

332

THE GETTYSBURG ADDRESS has been included, of late, in several anthologies of poetry—a sufficient proof that even anthologists are occasionally sound critics. It actually meets the major requirement of all poetry: it is a mellifluous and emotional statement of the obviously not true. The men who fought for self-determination at Gettysburg were not the Federals but the Confederates. Yet it took years for anyone to notice that Lincoln's sonorous strophes involved a plain misstatement of a fundamental fact.

333

RELIGION, of course, *does* make some men better, and perhaps even many men. There can be no doubt of it. But making them better by filling their poor heads with grotesque nonsense is an irrational and wasteful process, and the harm it does greatly outweighs the good. If men could be made better—or even only happier—by teaching them that two and two make five there would be plenty of fools to advocate that method, but it would remain anti-social none the less. If the theologians could only agree on their doctrines their unanimity might have some evidential value, just as the agreement of all politicians that the first duty of the citizen is to obey them and admire them has some evidential value. It may not be true, but it is at least undisputed by all save a small fraction of heretics, which is certainly something. Fortunately for common sense, the theologians are never able to agree. Even within the sects, and under the more rigid discipline, there is constant wrangling, as, for example, between the Jesuits and the Dominicans. Thus the cocksureness of one outfit is cancelled out by the ribald denial of all the rest, and rational men are able to consign the whole gang to statistics and the Devil.

334

The so-called Philosophy of India has found its natural home in Los Angeles, the capital of American idiots. Nowhere else, so far as I know, is there any body of theosophists left, and nowhere else has there ever been any substantial following for Yogi. All the quacks who advertise to teach Yogi in twenty lessons for $2, and all the high priests of the other varieties of Indian balderdash have their headquarters in Los Angeles, which is also the Rome of the American Rosicrucians.

335

The most steadily attractive of all human qualities is competence. One invariably admires a man who is good at his trade, whatever it must be—who understands its technic thoroughly, and surmounts its difficulties with ease, and gets substantial rewards for his labors, and is envied by his rivals. And in precisely the same way one admires a woman who, in a business-like and sure-handed way, has gone out and got herself a good husband, and persuaded him to be grateful for her condescension, and so made herself secure.

336

THE THEOLOGICAL argument by design, made popular in the
English-speaking countries by William Paley, is very far
from convincing. The Creator it adumbrates shows only a
limited intelligence compared to His supposed masterpiece,
man, and all save a few of His inventions are inimical to
life on earth rather than beneficial. There is nothing among
them that is at once as ingenious, as simple and as admi-
rably adapted to its uses as the wheel. I pass over the vastly
more complicated inventions of the modern era, many of
them enormously superior to, say, the mammalian heart.
And I also pass over the relatively crude contrivances of this
Creator in the aesthetic field, wherein He has been far
surpassed by man, as, for example, for adroitness of design, for complexity or for beauty, the sounds of an orches-
tra. Of the irrationality and wastefulness of the whole
natural process it is hardly necessary to speak. Nothing
made by man resembles it here, save only government. It is
hence no wonder that the overwhelming majority of men,
at all times and everywhere, have inclined toward the belief
that government is of divine origin.

337

LIKE all other forms of theology, Communism runs aground
on the fact that there are frequent bitter rows between
different factions of its prophets. Down to 1927 the American Communists believed in Trotsky's ideas as a cardinal
article of faith, almost on a par with the Christian's belief
in the Virgin Birth. But when Trotsky was knocked off he

became anathema, and soon his former customers were denying the validity of everything he said or had said, no matter how plausible. If he had begun arguing that 2 and 2 equalled 4 they'd have disputed it loudly, and denounced anyone who agreed as a scoundrel. Such disagreements tend to wreck all religions, even the simplest and most clearly outlined, for example, Mohammedanism, which has split into various warring sects, and indeed had done so so long ago as Omar Khayyám's time.

The one thing common to all prophets is their belief in their own infallibility. Their followers believe in it too, and so protestantism is an inevitable phenomenon in all religions. But it never actually produced reforms, or moves the central body of doctrine toward a greater plausibility. The Mohammedan sectaries, in fact, are even more idiotic than the body of orthodox Moslems, and in Christianity Protestantism is five times as imbecile as Catholicism.

338

BELIEVE what imbeciles believe, and the customers of quacks: they alone have the key to wisdom. There Communism and evangelical Christianity coincide. The hill-billies of Tennessee are taught that they know more about the operation of the world than Huxley, and the Communists are taught that they know more about economics than its professors, and far more than the bankers of Wall Street. This flattery of the imbecile is one of the essential devices of all religions, whether theological or political. He is made to believe that he has been admitted to an infallible arcanum, and so he gets the proud feeling that he is somehow superior to his betters. The Christian believes his secret and impeccable knowledge will admit him to a high seat in Heaven post-mortem, and the Communist believes that after tomorrow's revolution he'll have his betters by the tail.

339

ONE OF the evils of war is the fact that all gradations of opinion are abolished. Every imaginable act becomes either right or wrong. Thus war greatly prospers the natural imbecility of man. Its real drawback is not that it kills a few poor fellows, wounds a few more and destroys a great deal of property, for all of these things can be replaced very quickly: indeed, Napoleon I once said that his veterans could replace all the dead soldiers of France in one night. The real drawback of war is that it makes clear and honest thinking impossible. Even when the time of patriotic hallucination ends there is no return to sound logic, but simply to some new form of imbecility. Thus after the first two World Wars the American people took to believing that No. 3 and 4 could be prevented by signing treaties. This idea was quite as idiotic as those it displaced, and a great deal less appetizing.

340

THE COUNTRY high-schools of the United States no longer make any pretense to rational teaching. Now that every yokel above the intellectual level of an earthworm is run through them, their more intelligent teachers give up in despair, for not more than a small percentage of the pupils they face are really educable, at least beyond the fifth-grade level. The average curriculum shows a smaller and smaller admixture of rational instruction, and is made up more and more of simple time-killers. The high-school, in its earlier form of the academy, was a hard and even harsh school, but it actually taught a great deal. But in its modern form it is hardly more than a banal aggregation of social clubs. Every student of any pretensions belongs to a dozen—imitation fraternities, bands and orchestras, athletic teams, and so on. The most salient pupil, next to the champion athlete, is the female drum-major, proudly showing her legs, making the most of her budding breasts, and even offering the spectators a very good idea of the lines and foliage of her pudenda. The State universities are commonly required by law to take in, sight unseen, the graduates of these burlesque institutions of learning. As a result, they go downhill rapidly, and many of them are already burlesques themselves. As the student body increases in quantity it declines correspondingly in quality.

341

I KNOW a great many more people than most men, and in wider and more diverse circles, yet my life is essentially one of isolation, and so is that of every other man. We not only have to die alone; we also, save for a few close associates, have to live alone. I have been able, in my time, to give help to a good many young authors, male and female, and some of them have turned out very well. I often think of the immense number of others that I might have aided if I had only known of them.

342

IT IS the natural habit of pious people to take their religion much too seriously. When they demand universal respect for it, whatever its terms, they display a kind of vanity that is really laughable. This vanity, I suppose, is grounded on their belief that it will save their souls, and that they are thus superior to the damned. But why should any rational person be concerned about their souls? It is yet to be demonstrated that saving them would be of any practical benefit to the race in general.

343

THE THEORY behind representative government is that superior men—or, at all events, men not inferior to the average in ability and integrity—are chosen to manage the public business, and that they carry on this work with reasonable intelligence and honesty. There is little support for that theory in the known facts. The typical legislator is certainly not to be described rationally as a man of honor. On the contrary, it would be more accurate to describe him as a professional dishonorable man, for he cannot get into office without stooping. Superficially, the United States Senate looks to be an assemblage of free, able and conscientious men—the best club in the world. Actually, it is a gang of politicians who have reached their eminence by a long series of abject and discreditable acts. Even the best of them, at some point or other on his progress up the escalator, has crooked the knee to other politicians, most of them palpable rogues, and fawned over and flattered multitudes whose ideas are puerile. If he is intelligent at all he knows this, and the knowledge of it works a subtle corruption of his character. The President himself, basking in the White House, has been through the same dirty mill. He, too, has often said yes when he knew that no was right, and yielded supinely to the ignorance and prejudice of people not worth five minutes of an honest and honorable man's attention.

344

EVERY contribution to human progress on record has been made by some individual who differed sharply from the general, and was thus, almost *ipso facto*, superior to the general. Perhaps the palpably insane must be excepted here, but I can think of no others. Such exceptional individuals should be permitted, it seems to me, to enjoy every advantage that goes with their superiority, even when enjoying it deprives the general. They alone are of any significance to history. The rest are as negligible as the race of cockroaches, who have gone unchanged for a million years. It is not true, of course, that sub-human creatures are incapable of improvement: they may not will it, but natural selection often sees to it. Man, though he can will his own advancement, is suspicious of natural selection, and tries to circumvent it when it begins to operate upon his own species. Perhaps this is because he believes he is capable of devising safer and more effective methods of progress; perhaps it is only a testimony to his lingering subservience to theological ideas. Whatever the fact, he pays a heavy price for his resistance. It protects the superior, to be sure, but it protects the inferior even more. For one Darwin that it keeps alive, it preserves the lives of millions of poor dolts. Maybe the time will come when man will be sure enough of himself to let natural selection have its way—at least to a larger extent than now. When, as and if that time ever comes, the rate of human progress will be greatly accelerated.

345

IT IS not enough to take due care for the rights of the other fellow, for many of them are dubious and all of them are shifting; it is also necessary to take care for his dignity. This is the essence of good conduct. It is one of the foundation stones of life in human society.

346

THE IDEA that it is degrading for women to work in the fields is exclusively American. In all other civilized countries the farm women take their share of the lighter field tasks. That was true, also, in early America, as the ballad of "Maud Muller" shows. In those days even children raked hay, as you will find by examining the early schoolbooks. It has always been true, at least among colored folk, in the Cotton Belt.

In 1938 I made a long automobile tour through Germany in early harvest time. The women were all in the fields helping the men to get in the crops. The work was not hard, and certainly not for such sturdy women. I well remember how contented they all seemed, men and women alike, when they gathered in the middle of the afternoon for the *Kaffeepause*. The peasants of Europe make harvest a holiday, and when it is finished they invariably have a

party. Our American farm women have become sorry imitations of city women. They now wear the same clothes, and
have thus become unfit for the ordinary farm tasks. A great
many of them still tend gardens and milk cows, but it is
increasingly unusual to see them in the fields.

347

THE FUNDAMENTAL rights guaranteed by the democratic
theory, to wit, equality before the law, free speech and its
corollaries, and protection against governmental pretension
and usurpation, are by no means achieved by universal suffrage, which is not a right in itself, like the rest, but merely
a privilege. It does not follow that if the privilege were withheld the rights would be destroyed, or even invaded. On the
contrary, there is some evidence that they would be better
safeguarded than they are now, for the common man, while
he wants them for himself, is always reluctant to grant them
to others, and the demagogues he puts into high office are
their chronic enemies. The common people, in fact, are
far too stupid to decide between truth and falsehood, even
when their own welfare is at stake. If they could determine
such matters by vote they would probably make it official
doctrine that the earth is flat and that a horsehair put into
a bottle of water will turn into a snake. And if they had the
direct management of the socialized-medicine panacea they
would no doubt man it with chiropractors and patent-medi-
cine quacks, not with scientific physicians. Even though they
can't so decide they will probably contrive, soon or late, to
drive all really competent physicians off the staff, and substitute so-called ethical quacks. Many such quacks are al-

ready influential in the State and city health departments, in the Veterans' Bureau hospitals, and in the Public Health Service.

348

THE ARMY REGULATIONS provide that every man must be treated "so as to preserve his self-respect." This is the essence of conduct in civilized society.

349

IT ASTONISHED superficial observers to note how quickly and completely the majority of Germans swallowed the blather of Hitler, but there was, of course, nothing really surprising in it. They would have swallowed cannibalism just as fast if it had been advocated under the same conditions. Men in the mass will believe anything that promises to bring in the New Jerusalem, and the more idiotic it is the more eagerly they will embrace it. Nothing that is true ever convinces them. They demand illusion, and on the political plane they get it just as copiously as on the theological plane. It is difficult to imagine anyone having any real hopes for the human race in the face of the fact that the great majority of men still believe that the universe is run by a gaseous vertebrate of astronomical heft and girth, who is nevertheless interested in the minutest details of the private conduct of even the meanest man.

350

WHO ARE A's betters? They are all persons whom he envies, and with whom he would willingly change places. The essence of the superior man is that he is free of such envy.

Conscious of his capacity to survive and prosper within his own field, he has no desire to change places with anyone else, and hence he is incapable of envying anyone else. Thus he is inevitably a bad democrat, for democracy as a practical matter is based mainly and perhaps almost wholly on envy.

351

WHEN I hear a man applauded by the mob I always feel a pang of pity for him. All he has to do to be hissed is to live long enough. Remember the tragedies of Wilson and Roosevelt I. In their last days they were peeping sadly from the curtains like worn-out actors, as new and worse mounte-banks took their places. The mob is faithful only in its infidelity. It always stones those it has worshipped. Dewey of 1898 learnt that lesson, and Lindbergh after him. Hobson in his later years became simply a public mark. The mob didn't deign to hate him; it simply laughed at him. The old politician is always a sad and even a sort of tragic man. It would be humane to shoot all Presidents on the expira-tion of their terms, as I long ago proposed that every unsuc-cessful candidate for the Presidency be hanged. They dod-der along in a truly obscene manner, and always end as public nuisances. Al Smith was the perfect example.

352

THE GOOD humor of the American Negro is largely founded on cynicism. He is seldom deceived by the white folks who profess to love him, and his view of the race-leaders who prey upon him—for example, the clergy—is full of doubts and dubieties. I often wonder how many pious blackamoors really believe that they will turn into white angels post-mortem—probably no more than a few imbecile old women. The Negro spirituals, taking one with another, are anything but confident in tone, and after singing the most hopeful of them the congregation often turns to

> I went down the rock to hide my face;
> The rock cried out, "No hiding place,
> No hiding place down here."

353

In the long run, in all probability, my view of the history of the United States in my time will prevail—not, to be sure, on the levels of popular credulity, but on the higher and more rational levels. After all, that history will not be written exclusively by the authors of schoolbooks and the patriotic pedants of the American Historical Association: there will also be contributions from other and better sources, some of them not American at all. I believe that the intelligent view of American policy in the Roosevelt-Wilson-Roosevelt era will be substantially like the intelligent view of Roman policy in the last days of the Republic. That is to say, its honest purposes and sincere strivings will be almost obliterated by its endless knavishness and false pretenses. The United States got into both World War I and World War II by devices that would disgrace a gangster. Both times it made a foe by gross violations of elementary fair play, and both times its contribution to his overthrow consisted of stabbings in the back. It would be hard to imagine a course less glorious to a supposedly civilized nation. Nor would it be easy to imagine a more deliberate and disingenuous attempt to conceal the facts and poison judgment at home.

354

DEMOCRACY in the United States wars violently against the one real value that it offers, to wit, the enhancement of the dignity of the individual. It is always trying to reduce him to dependence and subservience. The more resolutely he tries to be his own man, the greater are his difficulties.

355

THERE seems to be a universal human tendency to make a virtue of faith—in Paul's give-away definition, "the substance of things hoped for, the evidence of things not seen." This madness prevails not only in the theological field, where it seems to have originated, but also in secular affairs. No American schoolma'am, male or female, ever seems to doubt that there is a mystical merit in believing whatever is officially promulgated. Indeed, the whole teaching process is grounded upon the inculcation of such balderdash. The man who presumes to question its basic postulates is almost unanimously regarded as a dubious fellow, and even when his doubts prevail he continues in limbo, as the case of Thomas Paine well exemplifies. As a matter of fact, he is the only sort of citizen, whether successful or not, whose existence is of any durable value to a presumably civilized nation. Faith in itself is certainly not a virtue; it is the very reverse of a virtue. It is a catch-all for every conspiracy against the plain facts. Worse, it leads inevitably to violations of everything rationally describable as sound morality. An individual who forces himself to accept this or that idea, or who pretends to accept this or that idea, not only on the ground that believing in it is an act of virtue but also on the ground that doing so is prudent is both a fool and a knave. Getting into Heaven by false pretenses is just as obnoxious to true decency as getting into a bank by false pretenses.

356

THE GENERAL unpopularity of the insurance solicitor is not hard to understand. As a solicitor *qua* solicitor he is certainly no worse than others; indeed, he tends to be superior to the general run. But in so far as he tells the truth about the uses of life insurance, he presses a moral duty on his customer, and so annoys him acutely. Also, he reminds his customer of death, and so annoys him again.

357

BUT YOU don't under*stand*! This answer of the Christian Scientist caught on a hook is always made by other merchants of blowzy metaphysical systems; for example, the Thomists. The Communists employ it constantly. Their first and often their only answer to a skeptic is to accuse him of not having read the Marxian gospels. If it turns out that he has, then they allege that he hasn't understood them. This, of course, may be true enough, for they are certainly hard to grasp; in fact, they consist in large part of very palpable nonsense. Not only are Marx's premises dubious; his logical processes are frequently worse, and so his conclusions seldom ring true. Metaphysics is almost always an attempt to prove the incredible by an appeal to the unintelligible.

358

IT IS a folly to try to beat death. One second after my heart stops thumping I shall not know or care what becomes of all my books and articles. Why, then, do I try to keep my records in order, and make plans for their preservation after I am an angel in Heaven? I suppose the real reason is that a man so generally diligent and energetic as I have been finds it psychologically impossible to resign the game altogether. I know very well that oblivion will engulf me soon or late, and probably very soon, but I simply can't resist trying to push it back by a few inches. Civilized man, indeed, is essentially indomitable. He refuses to yield to the natural laws that have him in their grip. His life is always a struggle against the inevitable—in Christian terms, a rebellion against God. I'll know nothing of it when it happens, but it caresses my ego today to think of men reading me half a century after I am gone. This seems, superficially, to be mere vanity, but it is probably something more. That something is a sound impulse—the moving force behind all cultural progress—to take an active hand in the unfolding of human life on this sorry ball. Every man above the level of a clod is impelled to that participation, and every such man desires his contribution to last as long as possible.

359

THE EFFORT to reduce the issues of World War II to a simple proposition in moral theology was precisely like the effort of the Prohibitionists to simplify the complicated and vexatious drink problem in the same way. It involved the same maudlin sentimentality, the same intellectual knavery, and the same fundamental idiocy.

360

IT IS beginning to be realized that trying to introduce cultural patterns by legislation is a hopeless business, but it is still believed more or less that they may be inculcated by education. Both beliefs, it seems to me, are evidences of a low degree of culture. Culture itself is neither education nor law-making: it is an atmosphere and a heritage—say that of the Renaissance or that of the pre-revolutionary Eighteenth Century. Take a boy from one cultural milieu and try to outfit him with the ideas, traditions, tastes and prejudices of another, and you succeed only in bewildering and demoralizing him. The new patterns of thought and feeling simply do not fit him: you have made him uncomfortable and unhappy in precisely the same way that tight shoes, high-waisted pants or scratchy underwear would make him uncomfortable and unhappy. He may learn to endure them, but they remain unnatural to him. The average American college, by teaching its students to be ashamed of their fathers, does not actually elevate them in the scale of culture. All it does is to make hollow snobs of them.

361

MODERATION in all things. Not too much life. It often lasts too long.

362

No MORE than one man in ten, at least in the United States, is really a master of the trade he practises. The rest take money for doing what they are quite incompetent to do, and thus live by false pretenses. For a good many years I had a lot to do with newspaper reporters. The percentage of genuine competents among them was considerably less than ten per cent. The rest were pathetically unfit for the every-day work of the craft. They lacked both the intelligence needed to unearth facts and weigh evidence and the elemental literary skill needed to make their findings intelligible. They were about as efficient, taking one with another, as so many one-armed paperhangers. In order to supply the deficiencies of one it was necessary to send out a second, and if the matter in hand was of any importance or delicacy it was usually necessary to send a third and a fourth. Later on I came into intimate contact with a large number of professional writers of a presumably higher grade—producers of short stories, poetry, articles, etc. Nine-tenths of them needed some help; indeed, many of them needed so much help that my struggles with their manuscripts spread the legend that I was trying to make all contributors to the *American Mercury* write alike. I had no desire to make them write alike, but my own way of writing was the only way I knew, and when theirs turned out to be impossible I had to substitute mine. The work of the world, in all departments, is chiefly done by bunglers. Very few generals are fit to be trusted with the lives of their troops, very few medical men are expert at diagnosis and treatment, and very few pedagogues really know anything about the things they presume to teach. As for clergymen, metaphysicians, politicians and other such frauds, it must be manifest that nearly all of them are completely incompetent. This incompetence, I suppose, is not to be held against mankind. Yahveh Himself set the example on the first six days.

363

THE PINK young pedagogues who used to leap out of the American colleges at frequent intervals, to the tune of loud outcries, always tried to make it appear that their radicalism had prevented their promotion. The facts really ran the other way. It was lack of promotion that made them radicals. When the New Deal came in it summoned thousands of them, and they had a chance to shine. But all that that golden opportunity achieved for them was to reveal their incurable inferiority. With power in their hands, they used it idiotically; with a free hand to execute their ideas at the taxpayers' expense, all they accomplished was to prove that those ideas were silly.

364

PENETRATING so many secrets, we cease to believe in the unknowable. But there it sits nevertheless, calmly licking its chops. Why is the so-called science of sociology, as ardent young college professors expound it, such an imbecility? Why is a large part of economics? Why does politics always elude the classifiers and theorizers? Why do fashions in metaphysics change almost as often as fashions in women's hats? Simply because the unknowable casts its black shadows across all these fields—simply because the professors attempt to label and pigeon-hole phenomena that are as elusive and intangible as the way of a man with a maid.

365

It seems to be hard for man to grasp the concept of impersonal causation; indeed, to all save a relatively small minority of men it is apparently almost impossible. The savage sees volition in every event of his environment—the blowing down of a tree, a stroke of lightning, the rise of a freshet, and all the diverse manifestations of disease. He simply cannot imagine anything happening without a conscious will behind it, and in the will he always sees a more or less rational purpose, usually thought of as malign. Civilized man, to some extent at least, has got rid of this primitive and all-embracing animism. If he is a Christian he still sees a Supreme Will in some of the most trivial happenings of his daily life, but even a Christian, supposing him to be reasonably enlightened, has learned to exclude that Supreme Will from many situations in which the savage and his own not distant forefathers saw it as predominant and undeniable. Thus he no longer looks for relief in prayer when he suffers an ordinary illness, but goes to a doctor instead, and is convinced that that doctor, even though an atheist, can offer him better help than the rector of his parish. And when he risks his money on some hazard, say a horse-race, and wants the best advice available, he no longer resorts to sticking a pin into a Bible or any other such device, but consults the dope-sheets instead, or follows a hunch that he seldom ventures to think of as divinely inspired. In very large part the transactions of his everyday life are carried on in this fashion, without any thought whatever of consulting or placating the powers of the air, and he ascribes their issue to natural causes, by which he means, in so far as he has reflected upon the matter at all, causes that do not involve any volition, and are thus not susceptible to deliberate starting or stopping.

The spread of such ideas has worked the greatest change ever recorded in the thinking of mankind, and hence in the pattern of human progress. But it should be noted at once that they are accepted even in part by only a relatively small minority of men, and in totality by no more than a tiny *corp d'élite*. The great majority still see volition in all really extraordinary events—say, the outbreak of war, a series of droughts, or the explosion of a volcano— and nine times out of ten they are inclined to ascribe that volition to extra-human personages, and to seek to change it by some scheme or other by propitiation. This fact explains the continued prosperity of religion in a world presumably grown rational. Its primary, and in many cases only, business is to appease the powers that can do man injury, and may be expected to do it whenever there is an insufficiency of flattery and bribes. More, even the highest varieties of man seem to have some difficulty in getting rid of the notion of volition when it comes to really massive events, inexplicable as yet in the sense that malaria, for example, is now explicable. They may laugh at the idea that a god causes the fall of a sparrow, but they back and fill a little when it comes to dealing with the revolutions of the spheres. Those revolutions remain inexplicable in the present state of science, and all that we can really say of them with any show of reason is that they are inexplicable, but there is a pressing tendency to explain them on the plan of the savage—that is, to ascribe them to the design and volition of some vasty and omnipotent power, wholly beyond imagination. Do the stars pursue their courses according to a more or less predictable programme? Then that programme must have been drawn up by some conscious agency, and the stars themselves and the whole universe with them must have been designed and fabricated by the same.

There is, of course, no support in either logic or evidence for this theory. All it shows is that modern man, despite the progress he has made, is still a blood brother to the savage, and prone on very slight provocation to return to his native animism. It moves; ergo, someone must be shoving it. But all that this syllogism really proves is that man is still unable to throw off altogether his primitive patterns of thought. What he must grasp at last, if he is ever to escape his immemorial bondage to brutal and irrational gods and devils, is the fact that the idea of causation does not necessarily involve the idea of a conscious cause. It may be, for all we know to the contrary—and the evidence pro is almost overwhelmingly impressive—that the universe is operated on a plan which does not call for the existence of any animating will at all—that it is purely impersonal and automatic, and has been so throughout all time. Will, as one notes it in man, may be no more than one of the chance by-products of the process, and as unimportant as, say, light. But how was this universe set spin-

ning? The answer may be that it was never set spinning—
that spinning has been one of the signs of its existence since
the beginning that was never a beginning, but simply a
state truly sempiternal.

Rather curiously, all the major religions and philosophical systems entertain the concept of an infinite future, and
multitudes of men seem to have no difficulty in grasping it,
but so far the race has steadily rejected—or perhaps more
accurately, overlooked—the concept of an infinite past. Yet
the latter, it must be manifest, is at least as plausible as
the former. Once man has taken it into his thinking—and
not before—he will cease to afflict himself with gratuitous
theories about the identity of the person or persons who set
the universe to spinning—theories that are not only gratuitous but also eternally vain, for even the most subtle of
them leaves unanswered the question as to who created the
original spinners. It will suffice for him, if he ever makes
that step, to note placidly that the universe moves, and that
it has been moving, apparently, for an infinite duration of
time. In other words, he will at last grasp the idea that volition is not necessary to causation. On this earth, in the
present state of human knowledge, will seems to be an important force, but the universe, for all we know, may be
operated on a system in which it is quite unknown. The
time may come when men will no more look for a conscious operator at its center than they now look for a con-
cious operator in a stick of dynamite.

366

THE THEORY seems to be that so long as a man is a failure he is one of God's chillun, but that as soon as he succeeds he is taken over by the Devil.

367

IT IS probably not possible to be quite content, save in early youth. When an individual begins to be authentically human, say at the age of ten, he begins to share in the common human talent for imagining a better world than the one he lives in, and after that his life becomes a constant but vain struggle against the inevitable and the irremediable. If he can manage to grasp the true nature of that sempiternal struggle—that is, if he can formulate the concept of the irremediable—then he reaches a sort of complacency and can get along comfortably enough. But not many men are ever able to conceive the irremediable, and even complacency is very far from contentment. The organism seems doomed to struggle idiotically until its last gasp. Its failure is inevitable, but it simply can't bring itself to admit the fact.

368

I USED to wonder why Woodrow Wilson was so excessively admired despite his palpable hypocrisy. Gradually the reason dawned on me. It is that hypocrisy is actually a kind of ideal in America. When the American cannot be really virtuous he becomes a hypocrite, and soon or late he convinces both himself and his neighbors that his hypocrisy is a sufficient surrogate for the virtue he lacks.

3 6 9

THE URGE to save humanity is almost always only a false-face for the urge to rule it. Power is what all messiahs really seek: not the chance to serve. This is true even of the pious brethren who carry the gospel to foreign parts. They are, with precious few exceptions, nonentities whose fate at home would scarcely carry them above the dignity of plow-hands or garage attendants, but in the wilds of Africa they are important persons, not only in their own view but also in that of the circumambient savages. They represent a new, mysterious and apparently extra-potent kind of magic; they have alms to give out; there are battleships behind them to protect them when they are menaced. All this is very caressing to their shabby egos. They realize the dream of every fifth-rate man, and prove his faith—that a change of job would shake off all his inferiorities, and make him a personage of dignity and puissance.

3 7 0

IT IS hard for man to grasp certain concepts—of impersonal causation, of the irremediable, of his own extinction. He therefore argues, with his head under his wing, that these concepts are inconceivable. But in this, obviously, there is nothing more than the sough of words. There are, no doubt, many more events and processes in the universe that man cannot grasp, and has so far failed even to imagine. Perhaps they are intrinsically and eternally beyond him, as life in the sun is beyond any organism based upon carbon molecules. But the fact that they are beyond him is no evidence, either pro or con. When they are described as unknowable everything that can be said about them has been said—and it is next door to nothing.

371

METAPHYSICS is the child of theology, and shows all the family stigmata. Both are based upon the theory that there is some mysterious magic in the unintelligible. Believing in it is thus an act of faith, lying precisely within the definition of faith by Paul in Hebrews XI, 1. This idea that there is something creditable about embracing nonsense is at the bottom of the vulgar idea that religion is a necessary part of the outfit of a decent man. It appears also on putatively higher levels, and is the hallmark of the whole race of so-called philosophers. A shining example was the late Paul Elmer More. He was a mid-Western yokel whose studies of Hellenism never quite emancipated him from the gospel-tent. He had a pious and solemn air, and thus acquired great influence in academic and other semi-ecclesiastical circles, but at bottom he remained a poor jackass. It would be hard to exaggerate the sophistry in some of his books. They were full of syllogisms so feeble that even professional metaphysicians must have been upset by them; indeed, not a few of them were so bad that they probably disturbed even professional logicians. I can't recall a single occasion on which he ever grappled realistically with an overt fact. He lived in the clouds, navigating a balloon made of an immense but empty baloney skin.

372

THE VANITY of man is quite illimitable. In every act of his life, however trivial, and particularly in every act which pertains to his profession, he takes all the pride of a baby learning to walk. It may seem incredible but it is nevertheless a fact that I myself get great delight out of writing such banal paragraphs as this one. The physical business of writing is extremely unpleasant to me, as it is to most other human beings, but the psychic satisfaction of discharging bad ideas in worse English is enough to make me forget it entirely. I am almost as happy, writing, as a judge is on his bench, listening with one ear to the obscene wrangles of two scoundrelly attorneys, or a bishop in his *cathedra*, proving nonsensically that God loves the assembled idiots.

373

IT IS often argued that religion is valuable because it makes men good, but even if this were true it would not be a proof that religion is true. That would be an extension of pragmatism beyond endurance. Santa Claus makes children good in precisely the same way, and yet no one would argue seriously that that fact proves his existence. The defense of religion is full of such logical imbecilities. The theologians, taking one with another, are adept logicians, but every now and then they have to resort to sophistries so obvious that their whole case takes on an air of the ridiculous. Even the most logical religion starts out with patently false assumptions. It is often argued in support of this or that one that men are so devoted to it that they are willing to die for it. That, of course, is as silly as the Santa Claus proof. Other men are just as devoted to manifestly false religions, and just as willing to die for them. Every theologian spends a large part of his time and energy trying to prove that religions for which multitudes of honest men have fought and died are false, wicked, and against God.

374

IT HAS been the rôle of the Russians in both of the great wars to save democracy to expose the falsity of the theory that the United States was fighting for it. The Czar as an ally in 1917 was certainly no more grotesque than Stalin as an ally in 1941. It is highly probable that the historians of the future will have a lot of fun with both alliances. After all, history is not written altogether by college professors. Occasionally there is a Gibbon or a Macaulay—and it is always the history of the Gibbon or the Macaulay that survives. What the professors write is taught to sophomores, but no one else pays much heed to it.

375

PERHAPS the most revolting character that the United States ever produced was the Christian business man. I speak of him in the past tense, for though he survives more or less in the South and the rural Middle West he has pretty well disappeared from the big cities. He was responsible even more than such gamblers as Jim Fisk and John W. Gates for the fact that business, once venerated by all right-thinking Americans, gradually became disreputable. His rapacity was quite as virulent as that of the early English factory-owners, and he was every bit as cruel. He fought to the end against any approach to rational and humane dealing with labor, and so opened the way for New Deal extravagances. His public position, which was still more or less honorable and envied in my boyhood, is now low indeed. Where he survives at all he is an object of suspicion. Let it appear in a criminal trial that the accused is a Sunday-school superintendent, and the jury says guilty almost automatically.

376

THERE is a considerable plausibility in the argument that religion serves a useful purpose in the world. It organizes large groups of men in cohesive associations, and pledges them, at least in their dealings with one another, to suspend some of the ordinary competitive motives. So long as they remain faithful to their church, they stand in opposition to the dog-eat-dog idea. They are men of "sanctified good will." Even revelation provides a brake on the wilder kinds of change. Revelations cannot be modified quickly, and so they tend to prevent constant revolutions. Unfortunately, the machine thus devised to halt heresy also tends to halt progress. It especially opposes itself to every projected change in moral ideas, and thus stands in the way of all rational dealing with them, and tends to exert a downright reactionary influence. But the obviousness of this demerit should not blind us to the fact that in other fields religion may really work some good, even although it may be completely absurd intrinsically.

377

IF ALL the farmers in the Dust Bowl were shot tomorrow, and all the share-croppers in the South burned at the stake, every decent American would be better off, and not a soul would miss a meal.

378

THE DOCTRINE that there are actually differences between races is well supported by the case of the American Indians. For a century or more they had every opportunity to embrace and adorn the American *Kultur*, with free education for the ambitious and social security for all. Yet they have not produced a single man of any genuine distinction in any field save military leadership, and even in that field, despite the opportunities thrown in their way, they have produced only a few. The Negroes, during the same time, have shown a very definite capacity for progress, though their opportunities have been much less. A few whites with some admixture of Indian blood have come to prominence on the old frontier, especially in politics, but all of them have been predominantly white, not Indian. Perhaps the flowers of this flock have been Robert L. Owen and Will Rogers, neither of them, it must be manifest, a really first-rate man. The Carlisle Indian School, maintained from 1879 to about 1930 for the training of likely Indians, produced a once famous football eleven, but not a single graduate of even the slightest distinction. Large numbers of its graduates, after their expensive education at the taxpayers' expense, returned to their tribes and became blanket Indians. In 1930 the Indian Bureau, convinced that the experiment of trying to turn Indians into useful Americans was a failure, closed the school, and took to educating its charges on a new plan, more consonant with their limited capacities. In brief, it has been found after long and costly experiment that the Indians cannot be brought into the American scheme of things. They apparently lack altogether the necessary potentialities. They differ from whites not only quantitatively but also qualitatively.

379

THE THEORY that all the races of mankind have descended from one stock is whooped up assiduously by the prophets of egalitarianism, but there is really no support for it in the known facts. On the contrary, there is every evidence that man emerged from the primordial apes in two or three or even four or five distinct races, and that they survive more or less to this day, despite the wholesale intermingling that has gone on in civilized countries. In many of the isolated backwaters of Europe—and of America too, as Appalachia witnesses—the traces of Neanderthal Man are much more evident than those of Crô-Magnon Man, who was vastly his superior. In any chance crowd of Southern Negroes one is bound to note individuals who resemble apes quite as much as they resemble Modern Man, and among the inferior tribes of Africa, say the Bushmen, they are predominant. The same thing is true of any chance crowd of Southern poor whites. It offers individuals so plainly inferior to the common run of Americans that it is hard to imagine them descending wholly from the same stock.

380

ONE OF the most irrational of all the conventions of modern society is the one to the effect that religious opinions should be respected. It is largely to blame, I suspect, for the slowness with which sound ideas are disseminated in the world. The minute a new one bobs up some faction or other of theologians falls upon it furiously, seeking to put it down. The most effective way to defend it, of course, would be to fall upon the theologians, for the only really useful defense is an all-out offensive. But the convention aforesaid protects them, and so they proceed with their blather unwhipped and almost unmolested, to the great damage of common sense and common decency. That they should have this immunity is an outrage. There is nothing in religious ideas, as a class, to lift them above other ideas. On the contrary, they are always dubious and often quite silly. Nor is there any visible intellectual dignity in theologians. Few of them know anything that is worth knowing, and not many of them are even honest.

381

IF A given man, A, is free to make his way in the world, then some other given man, B, must inevitably trail him and envy him. Despite a thousand New Deals it will be eternally impossible to equalize opportunity, for opportunity lies only in part in the external environment; the more important part is inside the man himself. The world is cold only to incompetent persons. Any college graduate who craves money—and nearly all of them count success in terms of dollars—may acquire it very readily by going home and writing another "Rosenkavalier," or inventing a new Peruna, or discovering a way to write editorials worse than any of those now printed. There is always a falsetto touch in complaints of lack of opportunity. They have been heard since the world began, but there has never been a time in history when a really smart fellow failed to get along.

382

No ONE ever heard of the truth being enforced by law. Whenever the secular arm is called in to sustain an idea, whether new or old, it is always a bad idea, and not infrequently it is downright idiotic.

383

WHY SHOULD religious ideas be considered somehow superior to other classes of ideas? Nine-tenths of them originated, after all, in nothing more noble than a yearning to placate the gods and keep out of trouble, and very few of them were launched by first-rate minds. All of the more successful religious leaders have been notoriously fools—for example, Paul of Tarsus, Mohammed, Martin Luther, John Calvin, Brigham Young and Mary Baker G. Eddy—and in the whole history of the world there is no record of one even remotely comparable to such a man as Newton or Goethe. Even Confucius fell far below that level. He was obviously superior to the average prophet of his time, but nevertheless his so-called wisdom, even at its best, remains of a relatively low potency. If there were times when he seemed to rise to the stature of Aristotle, there were other times when he didn't get much beyond the level of Martin Tupper.

The same thing is true even of Jesus. He rose, at rare moments, to real grandeur, but at other times the doctrine he preached differed very little from that now whooped from soap-boxes by Communists and other such simpletons. It is highly probable that some of His high points were not His own at all, but the contributions of later sages —for example, the magnificent colloquy with the woman taken in adultery in the Gospel of John. Even the Catholic exegetes now admit that its authenticity is dubious. Moreover, the tolerance that it inculcates is plainly at war with Jesus's position in like situations at other times.

384

IF, AS the fuglemen of democracy tell us, every man should have his fair chance in the world, then that chance should include freedom to demonstrate his superiority to the general, if he has any. Every scheme that puts a burden on the able and useful man as compensation to the inferior man, and especially any scheme that deprives him of his natural rewards in order to augment the income of the inferior man, is plainly grossly unfair, and a serious brake on progress. The most the inferior man deserves, on any rational scheme of public welfare, is a bare subsistence, and that subsistence ought to be predicated on his willingness to avoid any deliberate augmentation of his incapacity, say by begetting too many children. Anything more than that quickly resolves itself into robbing the competent in order to reward the incompetent. No juggling of words, however mellifluous, can ever conceal that purpose and effect.

385

THE IMMIGRATION of thousands of Southern hill-billies and lintheads to Baltimore after 1941, set up by the new war plants, had at least one good effect: it convinced native Baltimoreans that the Southern poor white was a good deal worse than the Southern blackamoor. Most Baltimoreans, before that time, tended to be Southern in their sympathies, but not many of them had any first-hand knowledge of the South. Thus my reports on the sub-Potomac proletariat, in my days of writing for the *Evening Sun*, were generally thought to be exaggerations. But when the poor whites began flocking in it was quickly seen that I had lingered behind the facts instead of going ahead of them. It was really shocking to Baltimore to discover that whites so thoroughly low-down existed in the country. They were filthier than anything the town had ever seen, and more ornery. The women, in particular, amazed it: they were so slatternly, so dirty and so shiftless that they seemed scarcely human. And it was plain at a glance that nine-tenths of their children were ill-nourished and diseased. In a little while the Baltimore cops were busy jailing the mothers of these forlorn brats for neglecting them so grossly that not a few were actually starving.

Detroit had already been wrecked by this metastasis from the South, but to Baltimore it was something new, and something alarming.

386

ANY EFFORT to adduce the miracles as proofs of Christianity must run aground on the Old Testament, for it describes the priests of other cults as capable of precisely the same wonders. In Exodus VII–X Moses, endeavoring to alarm Pharaoh into letting the children of Israel go, performs a long series of fearsome miracles before him, but Pharaoh's "wise men and sorcerers . . . also did in like manner with their enchantments," so the king was not convinced. There is no evidence in the text that the technic used by these sorcerers differed in any essential from that used by Moses and Aaron: indeed, it is clear that both used rods in their operations, apparently identical with the modern magician's wand. To be sure, Aaron's rod, turned into a snake, "swallowed up" the rods of the "wise men and sorcerers," but they must have had plenty in reserve, for in a few days they were once more hard at work, turning water into blood, creating multitudes of frogs, and so on.

387

POETRY differs from all the other arts in that no considerable specimen of it is ever thoroughly good. A lyric may be perfect, but nothing that is longer: in this Edgar Allan Poe was undoubtedly right. The plays of Shakespeare, though they swarm with magnificent passages, also show a great many spots of dullness and banality, and such a poem as Milton's "Lycidas" is very far from being *all* poetry. In music there is a much higher incidence of sustained merit— for example, the first movement of the Eroica symphony, that of Schubert's quintette in C major, and that of Brahms's first sextette. To be sure, these are not whole compositions, but they are at least as long as "Lycidas" or any act of "Hamlet" or "Macbeth."

388

DESPITE all the current gabble about curved space and other such phantasms, it is much easier to think of the universe as infinite than to think of it as having metes and bounds. If we try to think of it as finite we must somehow conjure up a region of sheer nothingness beyond its limits, and that is a feat I defy anyone to undertake. The human mind, in fact, simply cannot grasp the concept of nothingness. All we know of the universe tends to prove that it is unlimited, and the more we learn about it the more that impression is confirmed. Am I here, perhaps, citing a subjective reason to support an objective fact? Well, why not? What other reasons are there? We can examine the universe only through our senses, and our senses tell us that it spreads infinitely in all directions. By senses, of course, I do not mean the unaided senses of a child; I mean the enormously reinforced senses of a man of science. His telescope magnifies the evidence of his eyes, but what it tells him must still be recorded by his two optic nerves.

As for me, I refuse to waste thought upon a structure that apparently has no limits in either time or space. The human mind can imagine it, but that is as far as anyone can go. Our ordinary thinking constantly assumes temporal and spatial boundaries; indeed, we always think of objects and phenomena in terms of duration and extension. But there is no sign of either in the universe. We must either accept it as infinite, or stop thinking about it altogether. Any effort to put bounds to it, as for instance that of Einstein and his followers, leads quickly to plain absurdity. Curved space explains nothing whatsoever: it simply begs the question. Nor is there any genuine illumination in the general doctrine of relativity. It only says what every man of any sense knew before—that time and space are not absolute values, but only relative.

389

MAN's limitations are also visible in his gods. Yahveh seems to have had His hands full with the Devil from the start. His plans for Adam and Eve went to pot, and He failed again with Noah. His worst failure came when He sent His only-begotten Son into the world to rescue man from sin. It would be hard to imagine any scheme falling further from success.

390

MARX defined capitalism as ownership of the means of production. One man has the factory and another works in it. This is precisely the state of affairs in Russia. In this country the imaginative slave may at least hope, however vainly, to own a factory of his own some day; in Russia it is impossible. The theory, of course, is that the people in general own everything, but this involves a false definition of ownership. The title may be in them legally, but their bosses are perpetual lessees who exercise all their rights. To believe that Russia has got rid of capitalism takes a special kind of mind. It is the same kind of mind that believes that Jonah swallowed the whale.

3 9 1

THE REALLY unanswerable objection to Prohibition was always the Prohibitionists. If, in fact, they had believed honestly that forbidding rum to man would improve the world and had offered serious arguments for it, however unconvincing, most other men would have been disposed to listen to them politely. But it was quickly manifest that improving the world was the last consideration in their minds. What moved them was simply a violent desire to satisfy their egos by harassing their fellow-men. It quickly became apparent that Prohibition actually made the world worse, and yet they continued to be hot for it and, in fact, with increasing fervor. Toward the end they refused absolutely to hear any evidence against their delusion. They became mere brutal bullies, who, having discovered a way to work their will upon their betters, pursued it recklessly and relentlessly. The same thing is true of all other moral reformers. Their altruism is always only an afterthought. What really moves them is an insensate desire to wreak vengeance upon those who show superiority to them by being free of their delusions.

3 9 2

THE ANIMOSITY of metaphysicians to the common sense which informs the productive thinking of the human race is analogous to the animosity of Puritans to the natural and normal sexuality which keeps the race in being. In each case there is visible a distrust and fear of healthy biological functioning, an instinct of death.

393

NOTHING is easier than to induce men to be killed, provided only they be tackled in gangs. Taken one by one, the overwhelming majority of soldiers would probably run at the first fire, but thrown into battle *en masse* they almost always face wounds and death bravely. It is a manifestation of mass psychology that has never been sufficiently studied: no doubt there is some simple reason for it, now hidden beneath a mountain of illusion and false pretenses. In this matter of mass suicide there seems to be but little difference between nations. Even Greeks and Portuguese, properly trained and led, have been known to fight.

394

THE HIGHFALUTIN aims of democracy, whether real or imaginary, are always assumed to be identical with its achievements. This, of course, is sheer hallucination. Not one of those aims, not even the aim of giving every adult a vote, has been realized. It has no more made men wise and free than Christianity has made them good.

395

CHRISTIANITY, for all its wounds, is not likely to die; even its forms will not die; the forms, indeed, will preserve what remains of the substance. Of all religions ever devised by man, it is the one that offers the most for the least money to the average man of our time. This man may be very briefly described. He has enough education to make him view all religions somewhat critically, to make him competent to weigh and estimate them, particularly in terms of their capacity to meet his own problems—but not enough to analyze the concepts underlying them. Such an analysis leads inevitably to agnosticism; a man who once reaches the point of examining religions as psychological phenomena, without regard to their ostensible authority, always ends by rejecting all of them. But the average man is incapable of any such examination, and his incapacity not only safeguards his religion but also emphasizes his need of it. He must have *some* answer to the maddening riddle of existence, and, being unable to work out a logical or evidential answer, he is thrown back upon a mystical answer.

This mystical answer is religion. It is a transcendental solace in the presence of the intolerable. It is a stupendous begging of questions that nevertheless disposes of them. Of all such answers Christianity is at once the simplest and the most reassuring. It is protean and elastic; it has infinite varieties; it has comfort both for the man revolting despairingly against reason or congenitally incapable of reason, and for the man whose capacity for reason stops just short of intelligence. It is, at its best, a profound inner experience, a kind of poetry that is lived—call it Catholicism. It is, at its worst, a game of supernatural politics—call it Methodism. But in either case it organizes and gives a meaning to life. In either case it soothes the man who is too weak to stand up single-handed against the eternal and intolerable mysteries.

396

IT IS almost as dangerous to an author as to a politician to show a sense of humor, which is to say, a capacity to discover hidden and surprising relations between apparently disparate things, to penetrate to the hollowness of common assumptions, and to invent novel and arresting turns of speech. All dolts envy him this capacity, and hence dislike him. It took Mark Twain almost a generation to live down the fact that he viewed the world with laughing eyes. During his lifetime, save for a few years at the end, all the authorities whose judgment was relied upon at the time regarded him as somehow inferior to such dull fellows as Howells. Indeed, Mark himself yielded to that delusion, and it always amazed him when some literary anarchist began arguing that he was actually their peer. On the few occasions when he heard it maintained that he was not only their peer but their superior he was apparently genuinely shocked. Like any other man he was more or less a victim to the ideas of his time, though he devoted himself to deriding them. Up to a point he banged away at them, but then, of a sudden, they got him from the rear.

397

THE CHIEF difference between free capitalism and State socialism seems to be this: that under the former a man pursues his own advantage openly, frankly and honestly, whereas under the latter he does so hypocritically and under false pretenses.

398

THE CHRISTIAN way of life is a way that few men tread, and certainly no Christian. Even its old hortatory value is passing; we cannot even approximate it. What remains of it is poetry. It survives as a dream of what ought to be, or might be, but isn't. Thus moving into the limbo of the ideal, it takes on a new and greater beauty, as the Christian sacraments have taken on beauty as their literal significance has been gradually forgotten. The ethics of Christianity, beginning as the practical morality of a people so shrewd that they may be almost said to have survived extinction, will end as a Freudian wish. They will represent, not an order of daily conduct, but a vision of escape from life, an aspiration toward beatitude. Men will dream of embracing them as Hindus dream of achieving nothingness. A few inordinate men—ascetics, the spiritually gifted, idiots—will make the actual attempt, but the overwhelming majority of Christians, following the overwhelming majority of Hindus, will be content to throw a glance in that direction now and then, and maybe to heave a sigh and drop a tear.

399

NEXT to dancing, poetry seems to be the oldest form of art. It is, in its primitive forms, easier to make and easier to understand than any other artifact of the imagination. In the literature of every nation effective dithyrambs have always preceded sound prose. Indeed, prose comes late among the art forms, and plenty of nations have gone on for centuries without producing it at all. In the United States, despite the general cultural backwardness, there has been a relatively low output of memorable poetry, but that, I suppose, is due to the fact that the King James version of the Bible has supplied the appetite of the people in that direction. In no other country, not even Scotland, is the Bible read more assiduously, or turned to more often in times of storm and stress, when the consolations of poetry are needed. Most of the continental countries have been much less under its influence, largely, I suppose, because they have never had really living translations of it. The French Bible reads almost like an editorial in a newspaper. But the English Bible is overwhelmingly beautiful in the only two ways that poetry itself can be beautiful. That is to say, it is couched in mellifluous and memorable words and phrases, and it embodies a long series of eloquent statements of the obviously not true.

400

THE OLD concept of a Heaven flowing with milk and honey has been pretty generally abandoned by the more advanced wings of Christians; indeed, it is now resigned to Southern share-croppers and Mohammedans. The bliss of the saved is now reduced to the joy of living in the presence of Yahveh. This is supposed to be superior to the old wallowing in music and venery. It is, however, almost as imbecile. In essence it is simply the magnification of the ecstasy of a moron standing in the presence of a Truman or a movie star.

401

THE PSYCHOLOGY of the bore deserves a great deal more sober study than it has got. The prevailing view seems to be that mere stupidity is at the bottom of the yearning to annoy other people, but I believe that its true springs are to be found in an inferiority complex. A bore is simply a nonentity who resents his humble lot in life, and seeks satisfaction for his wounded ego in forcing himself upon his betters. The more those betters try to throw him off, the more persistent he is. This is certainly the case with the variety specializing in telephone calls. Tell one of them that you are just sitting down to dinner, or that the house is full of visitors, or that there is a fire nextdoor, and he will hang on doggedly. The only way to get rid of him is to say "I am sorry I can't talk to you" and then hang up. Even so, he is likely to call up again. An author is always horribly beset by such nuisances—writers of long holograph letters, idiots who send in manuscripts, askers of difficult questions, seekers of advice. I am usually polite to such poor fools, but now and then I have to slap down one of them brutally. In many cases, no doubt, their psychological inferiority amounts to mental disease. It is often difficult, in fact, to distinguish between a mere bore and a paranoiac.

4 0 2

IT IS one of the Christian delusions that Christianity brought charity into the world. It did no such thing. There were plenty of agencies for taking care of the poor and helpless long before Christianity was heard of, and even before Judaism. Both Christianity and Judaism have converted charity into a sort of pious racket. The alms-giver, in return for a trifling expenditure on this earth, will be rewarded with an infinity of bliss post-mortem. This purely selfish note is struck with great clarity by Judaism, and only less clearly by Christianity. It appears also in the other religions of the East. Thus religion has not really promoted charity, but debased it.

403

IT IS hard to read the history of the religious wars that once raged in Europe without getting a feeling that one is moving in a world of psychopaths. Why, indeed, should any sane person submit to being butchered on account of a puerile and unintelligible dispute over transubstantiation, the atonement, the immaculate conception or some other such metaphysical banshee? It does not surprise me, of course, to hear that the majority tried to exterminate the minority, for that is what the majority always does when it can. What I can't understand is that the minority should have submitted to the slaughter, voluntarily and almost gladly. Even in the worst persecutions known to modern times—say, those of the Protestants in France in the Sixteenth Century—it was always possible for a given member of the minority to save his hide by going to mass and having his children baptized by a priest. A Protestant who was willing to consent to that harmless mumbo-jumbo, even in the days of Catherine de' Medici, went quite unmolested, and his descendants today are respectable members of the Gallican Church, which is to say, skeptics. Well, then, why did so many of the Huguenots refuse? Why did they choose to be robbed, mauled and murdered?

The answer given by Protestant historians is that they were a noble people, and preferred death to heresy. But this merely begs the question. Is it actually noble to cling to theological ideas in so cocksure a manner? Certainly it doesn't seem so to me. After all, no human being really *knows* anything about the transcendental matters with which all religions deal. The most he can do is to follow one leader rather than another, or to match his private guess against the guesses of his fellow-men. For anyone to say absolutely, in so murky a field, that this or that notion is wholly and irrefragably true and that or this other one is utterly false is simply to talk buncombe. Personally, I have never encountered a religious idea—and I especially do *not* except the idea of the existence of God—that was instantly and solidly convincing, as, say, the Copernican cosmography is convincing. But neither have I ever encountered a religious idea, at least above the level of the Holy Rollers and other such savages, that could be dismissed offhand as quite unthinkable. The fact that it is not unthinkable is proved by the fact that presumably sane and civilized men have thought it, though I should add at once that I have never done so myself. Is it true that *Homo sapiens*, at the final failure of his wind, throws off an impalpable emanation, and that this emanation, if he has been guilty of blasphemy, fornication or Sabbath-breaking on earth, will be boiled for endless ages in a cauldron of pitch? Surely it seems highly improbable, and my private inclination is to set down anyone who believes it as a credulous ass, but it must be manifest that its improbability stops at $\infty - x$, and is thus appreciably short of complete impossibility. Of all the Presidents of the United States not more than half a dozen have refused definitely to believe it, and of the military heroes of the country, no more, if indeed as many.

In view of this uncertainty—at least in the present backward state of mankind—it seems to me to be vanity or worse for any man to cling to his religious ideas, whatever they may be, too tenaciously, or to submit to any inconvenience on account of them. Far better for him to conceal them discreetly, or to change them as the hallucinations of the majority change. My own theology, being wholly skeptical and hence tolerant, is doubly offensive to the subscribers to practically all other systems, but at the moment, by an accident of American political history, they are forbidden to punish me for not agreeing with them. At any moment, however, some group or other among them may seize the power to do so, and proceed against me in the classical manner. If that ever happens I give notice here and now that I shall get converted to their whim-wham instantly, and so retire to security and peace with my right thumb laid against my nose and my fingers working like those of a cornetist. I'd even do it today, if there were any practical advantage in it.

The answer to such considerations, as made by believers, is almost always an appeal to sentimentality—in other words, an attempt to strike below the logical belt. I am asked to state categorically whether or not I respect and venerate the martyrs who have died gloriously for the faith. My answer is no. A martyr, by my lexicography, is on all fours with a fool who risks and loses his life in any other showy but useless way—say, a man who lifts the tail of a mule and then inserts a straw into the animal's hawse-pipe. It may be brave, but it is certainly not sense. I am more familiar than most with the history of the martyrs, but I can't recall a single one who died for an idea that was indubitably true, and has remained true to this day. All of them went to their unpleasant deaths mouthing palpable nonsense. The same thing, alas, must be said of the heroes who have died in battle, fighting for this or that brand of political idealism. If one crowd of them died for what was true, then the other crowd must have died for what was false, which at once reduces the stock of military martyrs by 50% Moreover, there is never any general agreement as to which side was right and which wrong, and in consequence the title of the former is clouded—and by evidence precisely as good as that which supports them. Dying for ideas, in fact, is a bad way to propagate them, even among believing minds. It is a great deal safer, more rational and more effective to live for them. But even living for them, in a world so sadly abandoned to imbecility, is less comfortable than trying to live in spite of them.

404

THE TROUBLE with the theologians is that they are very adroit logicians, and so usually prove too much. If the existence of man proves that of God, on the commonly stated ground that every effect must have a cause, then the existence of God equally proves the existence of some super-God, and so on *ad infinitum*. Theologians have made many efforts to meet this dilemma, but never with success. They have been quite unable to imagine a power creating itself, just as all the rest of us have been unable to imagine it. They pretend otherwise, but their pretense is quite transparent.

405

THE ESSENTIAL dilemma of education is to be found in the fact that the sort of man (or woman) who knows a given subject sufficiently well to teach it is usually unwilling to do so. There are, of course, exceptions, but they tend to be confined to the higher levels, where even the most aloof savant may usually be prevailed on to take a few apprentices. His motive may be bad—in the average case, in fact, it is simply a desire to get some free helpers in his own work—but nevertheless he commonly makes a more or less diligent effort to instruct his pupils, if only because it increases their value to him, and he would be disgraced to have ignoramuses claim him as their master. But on the lower levels the average teacher really knows little about the thing he presumes to teach; he is simply a pedagogue. In the public schools, in fact, and also in the private schools, it is common to shift him from one subject to another, though they may lie miles apart, or to load him with two or three or more that have nothing in common. Savages order this business better. The teaching of the young, in most tribes, is handed over to the leading men thereof. They are not pedagogues at all, in the civilized sense; they are rather men who happen to know. It may be objected that what they teach is mainly a series of customs and superstitions that have no support in the overt facts, but to that two answers may be made. The first is that these customs and superstitions, whatever their objective dubiousness, at least have validity and value for the young of the tribe, and the second is that the schoolteachers of civilization seldom inculcate any ideas that are clearly more rational.

4 0 6

SAMUEL JOHNSON'S saying that patriotism is the last refuge of scoundrels has some truth in it, but not nearly enough. Patriotism, in truth, is the great nursery of scoundrels, and its annual output is probably greater than that of even religion. Its chief glories are the demagogue, the military bully, and the spreaders of libels and false history. Its philosophy rests firmly on the doctrine that the end justifies the means—that any blow, whether above or below the belt, is fair against dissenters from its wholesale denial of plain facts.

4 0 7

THE JEWISH theory that the *Goyim* envy the superior ability of Jews is not borne out by the facts. Most *Goyim*, in fact, deny that the Jew is superior, and point in evidence to his failure to take the first prizes: he has to be content with the seconds. No Jewish composer has ever come within miles of Bach, Beethoven and Brahms, no Jew has ever challenged the top-flight painters of the world, and no Jewish scientist has ever equalled Newton, Darwin, Pasteur, or Mendel. In the latter bracket such apparent exceptions as Ehrlich, Freud and Einstein are only apparent. Ehrlich, in fact, contributed less to biochemical fact than to biochemical theory, and most of his theory was dubious. Freud was nine-tenths quack, and there is sound reason for believing that even Einstein will not hold up: in the long run his curved space may be classed with the psychosomatic bumps of Gall and Spurzheim. But whether this inferiority of the Jew is real or only a delusion, it must be manifest that it is generally accepted. The *Goy* does not, in fact, believe that the Jew is better than the non-Jew; the most he will admit is that the Jew is smarter at achieving worldly success. But this he ascribes to sharp practises, not to superior abilities.

408

THE CHRISTIAN concept of God is one more proof that Christianity is essentially an oriental religion. Heaven is a place in which the highest reward of the faithful will be simply admission to the Presence of the Most High. This is a completely Asiatic notion: admission to the Presence is a signal of favor. Another oriental concept is government by whim. No one can search the heart of God, or know His motives: it is sufficient that some souls are smiled on, and others frowned on. Thus the practises of an oriental court are carried over into the immortal realm. The concept of Limbo is of the same general type. Children are innocent, but they have not yet earned the right to bask in the Presence.

409

IT SEEMS to me to be perfectly imaginable that there may exist orders of intelligence as far superior to that of man as that of man is above the intelligence of a dog; or that of a dog is above that of, say, an earthworm; or that of an earthworm is above that of, say, a bacillus. Here there are plain differences, not only quantitatively, but also qualitatively.

But mankind almost always insists on picturing God as only a greatly magnified man. He is thus endowed with all the puerile weaknesses of man, and the notion of His omnipotence becomes absurd. This absurdity lies at the heart of Christianity. It is completely inconceivable that a really omnipotent God would have been forced into the childish device of sending his Son to save His own creatures. He could have saved them by simply willing it, and the miracle would have been no greater in any sense than the miracle of impregnating a virgin—which, in fact, may be feasible soon in the laboratory.

Having this nonsense at its heart, Christianity is not hospitable to clear thinking, and its whole history has been a history of combats with rational ideas. If it had started off, like some of the other Eastern religions, with a God completely unimaginable and superhuman, it would have been more persuasive to civilized man. As it is, it has lost ground in proportion as man has come to reflect seriously and effectively about the universe. If God be imagined as a creature with an order of intelligence entirely different from and superior to that of man, the whole question as to who created God loses some of its force, for it is entirely conceivable that God's intelligence may be sufficient for self-creation. In brief, once we admit that there is a kind of intelligence entirely different from that of human beings, we can credit it with any powers that seem necessary and still escape absurdity. But when that intelligence is depicted or thought of as substantially identical to human intelligence, all its miracles become incredible. Even the moral system of the Christian God is dubious. Reduced to its essentials, it is simply the moral system of any somewhat fussy Presbyterian. It is absurd to ask civilized man to revere such a donkey.

410

CARLYLE, in his "Heroes and Hero-Worship," reviled Napoleon for believing "too much in the dupeability of men." This is another of Carlyle's exceedingly shaky judgments. Napoleon never actually overestimated that dupeability. So far as I am aware, in truth, no man on this earth has ever done so. The capacity of human beings to believe the obviously not true is apparently almost unlimited. Politicians fall into trouble, not by overestimating it, but by underestimating it.

411

THE EFFECTS of mere luck upon human destiny are always greatly underestimated. It is luck that is really responsible for everything that the anti-Sumnerian sociologists ascribe to environment. Indeed, environment, as they think of it, is nothing more than luck, and so, for that matter, is heredity. If a man is born with good natural parts the fact is simply what the insurance policies call an act of God, and if he is thrown into a favorable environment it is the same precisely. Unhappily for the peace and security of mankind, it is almost impossible for one man to view another's luck objectively, without reading into it some sort of subjective viciousness. The lucky man is universally regarded by the luckless with a hostile eye, and he himself always inclines to see something akin to depravity in their ill fortune. To him, nine times out of ten, they are simply lazy, just as he himself, to them, is simply anti-social.

This potency of mere luck stands eternally against all the fine dreams of theoretical democracy. Even professed democrats have begun to see that equality of ability is a chimera, but most of them still cling to the idea of equality of opportunity. Opportunity, however, is determined by luck quite as plainly as ability. No laws, however adroitly drawn, can ever equalize it. No scheme of looting the lucky can ever dispose of it. It will continue to divide men into haves and have-nots until the end of time. No matter what burdens and penalties are piled upon the lucky man, and no matter whether his luck comes by nature or by nurture, he will continue to enjoy an advantage over the poor fish.

412

SCIENCE, at bottom, is really anti-intellectual. It always distrusts pure reason, and demands the production of objective fact. The so-called philosophers who still survive in the world (just as fortune-tellers and witch-doctors survive) argue that a scientist cannot carry on his business without some grounding in metaphysical theory, but for this there is no evidence whatsoever; on the contrary, the career of almost any competent scientifico proves that it is false. All the metaphysical equipment he really needs is contained in common sense, and he shares it with carpenters and bricklayers. Whenever he steps beyond it he gets into difficulties, and very often he comes dramatically to grief. Some of the great glories of science, including many who have adorned the non-physical sciences, have been as innocent of metaphysical theory as so many police lieutenants. The business of a man of science in this world is not to speculate and dogmatize, but to demonstrate. To be sure, he sometimes needs the aid of hypothesis, but hypothesis, at best, is only a pragmatic stop-gap, made use of transiently because all the necessary facts are not yet known. The appearance of a new one in contempt of it destroys it instantly. At its most plausible and useful it simply represents an attempt to push common sense an inch or two over the borders of the known. At its worst, it is only idle speculation, and no more respectable than the soaring of metaphysicians.

413

DEMOCRACY, in the last analysis, is only a sort of dream. It should be put in the same category as Arcadia, Santa Claus and Heaven. It is always a mistake to think of it as a reality. It never really exists; it is simply a forlorn hope.

414

THE BELIEF that man is outfitted with an immortal soul, differing altogether from the engines which operate the lower animals, is ridiculously unjust to them. The difference between the smartest dog and the stupidest man—say a Tennessee Holy Roller—is really very small, and the difference between the decentest dog and the worst man is all in favor of the dog. There have been Christian theologians observant enough to note these facts, but I know of none who has had sufficient candor to grant the necessary implications. Cornered, they usually fall back upon the contention that man is the only creature able to contemplate and fear death. But is this really true? If I pursue a cockroach across the kitchen floor, seeking to tread out his life, what is it he runs from, the menace of death or only the menace of injury? If he can formulate the concept of injury, then what reason is there for believing that he can't formulate the concept of fatal injury? I do not assert positively that this proves that he has any coherent idea of the nature of death, but neither has the average human being. When the Holy Roller says that he fears it what he means is that he fears the unpleasant possibilities which his pastor tells him may follow it. This, obviously, is not rational thought, but simply delusion. The rest is only the elemental biological resistance to extinction, common to all living creatures, even the amoeba.

4 1 5

MY OLD plan to print an essay entitled "Proposals for Improving the Design of the Human Frame" may still be worth developing. Getting the materials together might be troublesome, but nevertheless it would not be impossible. The manner in which human eggs, after their production in the ovary, are thrown out into space, and then painfully recovered by the tentacles of the fallopian tubes, is really a magnificent proof of the imbecility of whoever designed the human body.

The case of the teeth is also full of difficulties for the argument by design. It is obvious that they should be as durable as possible, but it is equally obvious that their durability is very small. Perhaps the initial mistake of the Creator lay in grounding the whole plant and animal world upon a series of carbon compounds, all of them extremely unstable. If silicon had been chosen instead, or, better still, platinum, there would have been a far different story to tell. Incidentally, it is possible that this has been done in some other planets, and that life thus exists in places where human biologists, made of carbon themselves, believe it to be impossible. Even scientific men cannot quite rid themselves of viewing the whole universe in anthropomorphic terms. They constantly assume, for example, that life cannot go on without oxygen, despite the plain fact that many bacteria *do* live without it.

416

If RELIGION really made men better, then the Catholics of the immigrant groups, trained in parochial schools and under strong priestly influence, ought to be extraordinarily virtuous, but there is no evidence that they are. All the statistics that I am aware of indicate that they supply as many recruits to the prisons and reformatories, proportionately, as any other class of white Americans. Nevertheless, it is hard to believe that the exhortations and admonitions of their pastors have no effect whatever, so it naturally follows that they must be appreciably more vicious, at bottom, than Protestants, Jews and infidels. But are they in fact? I know of no official evidence either pro or con. The Irish, once abnormally turbulent, are now thoroughly housebroken, and Irish criminals become rare. The Germans never supplied any abnormal number; indeed, they have always been described as law-abiding. This leaves the Italians and Slavs. I suspect that most of the current Catholic evil-doers come from that direction. The Italians were in the forefront of the fray during the barbaric days of Prohibition, and the Poles seem to be hotheaded and contumacious. It is not unusual, in fact, for them to rough one of their own priests. Thus his whooping up of righteousness has very little force and effect.

417

OF ALL the varieties of biography perhaps the most unreliable is the kind based on letters. It is rare, indeed, for a man to reveal himself, honestly and completely, to his correspondents. An account of me, based upon my thousands and thousands of letters to all sorts of persons, mainly strangers, would leave out nine-tenths of my story. It would offer only occasional glimpses of my true thoughts, and in large part it would omit even my overt acts. A man seldom puts his authentic self into a letter. He writes it to amuse a friend or to get rid of a social or business obligation, which is to say, a nuisance.

Autobiography, of course, is something else again. Every man writes most willingly and hence most entertainingly when writing about himself. It is the one subject that engrosses him unflaggingly, day in and day out. To be sure, he almost invariably lies when he undertakes it, but his lying is of a species that is not hard to penetrate. One quickly learns what sort of impression he is trying to make, and after that it takes only a reasonable acumen to discount his evidence sufficiently. He can never quite fool a really smart reader. But his false pretenses, when detected, do not spoil the interest of his story; on the contrary, they add to that interest. Every autobiography thus becomes an absorbing work of fiction, with something of the charm of a cryptogram.

418

MORAL certainty is always a sign of cultural inferiority. The more uncivilized the man, the surer he is that he knows precisely what is right and what is wrong. All human progress, even in morals, has been the work of men who have doubted the current moral values, not of men who have whooped them up and tried to enforce them. The truly civilized man is always skeptical and tolerant, in this field as in all others. His culture is based on "I am not too sure."

419

ART FORMS have their infancy, their heyday and their decline. The symphony, I suspect, is on its way out, and may soon be as archaic as the fugue. I do not mean that it will disappear altogether, any more than the fugue has disappeared altogether, but it will cease to be the dominant orchestral form. The old-time opera may be going the same way, and probably is. The opera of the future, if opera survives at all, will differ from it even more than the Wagner music-drama differs from it. In the other arts the same transition is apparent. It is more than a little likely that oil painting is going out, and along with it the novel. There are plenty of painters and novelists left today, but it must be manifest that they are not producing anything comparable to the masterpieces of former days. Many of them equal, or even excel the old masters in technical skill, but they somehow fail to get any great passion into their works. The essay as Addison and Lamb knew it is now dead: its last practitioner in America was Agnes Repplier. But new forms of short prose are appearing all the time, and one of them, in the near future, may take the place of dominance that the old-time essay had up to a century ago.

420

CHRISTIANS can no longer claim a monopoly of virtue. Their pretensions in that direction were plausible enough so long as the great majority of decent people in Christendom were believers, but this is by no means the case today, and fair men have begun to observe that, taking one man with another and one day with another, non-Christians really tend to be more decent than Christians. Any moral system that excludes supernatural authority is apt to be better than one that takes it in, if only because it lays heavier stress on the sanction of reason and is in closer contact with the sanctions of human nature.

Such men as Archbishop Curley of Baltimore or Bishop James Cannon, Jr., if non-Christians, would have been denounced as scoundrels by all Christians. At the time of his row with the Baltimore *Sun* Curley's conduct was really infamous. He seemed to be quite without any concept of decency or honor or common fairness. The same might have been said of Cannon, though I incline to believe that he was an appreciably better man than Curley. Both may be described briefly as pious bounders.

421

ACCORDING to American theory, all power is in the hands of the plain people, and according to American legend they always exercise it wisely. The theory, of course, is almost as absurd as the legend. The plain people, in fact, can only exert their power through agents, and in the election of those agents they seldom face a clear choice between a good candidate and a bad one, or a wise idea and a foolish one. In the normal case both candidates are frauds and both ideas are idiotic. Thus the great shifts in American opinion that are witnessed from time to time are not commonly of any genuine significance. It would be very hard for an impartial historian to discover what was gained for common sense and common decency when the government by men of money prevailing from the Civil War to 1932 was overthrown at last, and a government by labor leaders and social workers substituted. The taxpayer, in fact—and every citizen is a taxpayer, whether he realizes it or not—found himself in a worse situation than he had been before, and it is highly probable that, in the long run, even the common workman will find that he lost a great deal more than he gained.

422

THE ORDERS of the innumerable Dogberries mobilized at Washington by the New Deal were seldom defensible in logic or on the known facts, and not unseldom they were extraordinarily arbitrary and oppressive. This was true also of the mandates of the lesser Dogberries in office in the States. Their wanton character caused a great deal of public discontent, and also some pained public speculation. Why was there so little apparent regard for the general convenience, or even for the general welfare? The answer, it always seemed to me, was quite simple. Give an inferior man absolute power over his betters, and he will use it harshly.

Very few of the Dogberries, high or low, had been men of any genuine dignity or authority before they were given office by presidential fiat. For every one who had been in a responsible position, won by experience and ability, there were at least fifty who had been college tutors, charity racketeers, unsuccessful lawyers, petty jobholders, and other such nonentities. The grand master of them all, Harry L. Hopkins, had been a money-cadger, first for various minor charity rackets in New York, then for the Red Cross, and then for the New York Tuberculosis and Health Association. It was simply not in human nature for such ignoble fellows, once they had the club of government in their hands, to refrain from using it recklessly. The wonder is, indeed, that they ever showed any moderation at all.

4 2 3

THE ESSENTIAL part of the test set up for jurors and witnesses in Article 36 of the Maryland Declaration of Rights is not the simple belief in "the existence of God" required of office-holders in Article 37, but belief in a scheme of divine rewards and punishments. The juror or witness must believe that God rewards the virtuous and punishes the sinful, "either in this world or the world to come." It must be plain that, once this is subscribed to, the whole judicial process becomes vain. Why should judges and juries undertake to do what God will do? Why should the accused be forced to submit to double jeopardy?

No Christian sect actually believes in divine justice. All advocate secular punishments, and most of them even advocate such punishments for heresy. None will undertake to say categorically that this or that man will go to Heaven, or to Hell. No Catholic bishop would dare to say of me, for example, that I am certainly doomed, though he might very well believe it probable. The system of divine justice that he cherishes is so loose and ineffective that he can imagine that even Pope Alexander VI may have escaped the fire. Nor is he sure that even the virtuous popes got to Heaven. Popes, indeed, have to confess their sins precisely like laymen, and so do the most austere Trappists and the most innocent nuns.

4 2 4

EVERYTHING considered, perhaps the best job in Christendom today is that of a bishop. All secular functionaries are exposed to the whims of mobs, but a bishop, once consecrated, is almost bullet-proof: even armed uprisings commonly leave him unscathed. He is well-paid, pleasantly entertained, highly respected, free from mundane cares, and in many ways above the law. If he wants to take a day, or a week, or a month off, he simply puts on his shovel hat and goes. If the mood strikes him to horn into a civilized dinner, with good cigars and sound wine, he intimates as much to some opulent and far-seeing layman of his diocese, and the birds go on the fire. If he is delivered of public remarks, however banal, the newspapers report him respectfully. If, on a gray day in Winter, he is annoyed by his valet's knock at 7 a.m., he shoves the clock back, and sleeps until noon. If he dislikes anyone, all he has to do is to excommunicate him. If he needs money, he simply arises in his cathedral and preaches upon Dives.

Altogether, a free, spacious and lordly life, full of ease, honor and contentment. Even atheists admit that a bishop is somebody. I try not to envy anyone in this world, but whenever I think of any bishop of my acquaintance, and contrast his voluptuous *dolce far niente* with my own hard lines, I find it very difficult to chase away a green cast that sicklies o'er my gills.

425

THE SO-CALLED proletarian authors made the capital mistake of trying to convert abject and ignominious persons into noble characters. This is the weakness in John Steinbeck's "The Grapes of Wrath." The actual proletarian is never a hero. He is not even the hero of a proletarian revolt, which is invariably operated by superior persons from the upper strata. The proletarian is by definition an incompetent and ignominious fellow.

426

A RATIONAL educational system would require all women who teach boys to be married. There are obvious dangers in putting spinsters in authority over healthy young males. Spinsters, indeed, are probably undesirable teachers even for young girls. I incline to believe that men teachers should be married too, or at least that they should be persons of some worldly experience. They have enough inhibitions as it is, without adding those of sex. There is a very high percentage of homos among them. They fall for all the current manias. In the days of Prohibition the *Literary Digest* polls showed that more schoolteachers were in favor of it than any other class. Our young are thus thrown into

the hands of eunuchs, male and female. The whole attitude
of these eunuchs is false and unhealthy. They see the world
through distorting glasses, and are full of delusions. The
ideal educator would be a genuinely superior man, for the
boy who comes into contact with such a man invariably
picks up something valuable. Unfortunately, it is impossible to induce superior men to teach. The best we can do
is to call in those who, while generally inferior, at least have
a sufficiency of common sense to be free from the more absurd of current hallucinations. In the Catholic schools the
matter must be even worse than it is in the public schools.
In some ways these Catholic schools are superior to the
public schools, but I believe that on the whole they are
quite as bad. Not only do they waste a great deal of their
time and energy inculcating the imbecilities of theology;
they are also staffed by people who are either psychopathic
cases or childish innocents. Their lack of good sense is
bound to have a bad effect on their pupils.

427

OBVIOUSLY, some sort of force keeps the universe spinning,
and in the absence of any knowledge whatsoever as to its
character it is not unnatural for multitudes of men to think
of it as a kind of intelligence. This easy animism is congenital in mankind, and it will probably be many centuries before even the most enlightened men throw it off altogether.
But if we try to think of the prime mover of the universe as
an intelligence, we are quickly brought up by evidence that
it must be a very inferior intelligence. In many ways, indeed, it shows marked inferiority to man, presumably its

creature. It has a certain cleverness, but not as much as he
has. Its designs are inferior, and its execution is clumsy,
wasteful and not infrequently preposterous. If it has any
moral sense, then that moral sense must be represented by
something closely approaching a vacuum. Any man who
was so completely brutal would be looked upon with horror
by all other men.

428

THE Pure Food and Drugs Act, which is sound in principle, for it is undoubtedly a proper function of government
to protect people against impostures that they cannot penetrate themselves, is gradually falling into the hands of up-
lifter-bureaucrats, and soon or late its enforcement is bound
to become arbitrary and oppressive. I believe that it should
be limited to requiring that everything for human ingestion
that is offered for sale should show a label indicating its
ingredients, and giving information about its degree of
purity. A difficulty lies in the fact that, in the case of drugs,
and also in that of preservatives, the average man is puzzled
by chemical terminology, and has no ready means of inter-
preting it. I think that this might be got round by requiring
that the name of every dangerous ingredient be printed in
red ink, or with some other arresting notice that its use is
hazardous. Such details are certainly not beyond the ingenuity of really intelligent officials, if any exist. But I have
some doubt that the police power should be carried further.
A fool who, after plain warning, persists in dosing himself
with dangerous drugs should be free to do so, for his death
is a benefit to the race in general. In the same way he
should be free to resort to quacks when he is ill. In the days

when the Maryland Legislature was considering a bill forbidding Christian Scientists to practise in the State I opposed it, though such medical dignitaries as Dr. William W. Welsh supported it. I argued, first, that enforcing it would be impossible, and second, that persons idiotic enough to take Christian Science treatment for dangerous diseases should be allowed to do so—that their departure for bliss eternal would be good riddance. The truth of my first contention has been amply proved by experience. The act is still theoretically in force, but Christian Science healers still swarm in Baltimore. It is rare, indeed, for one of them to be hauled up, and then he nearly always escapes punishment.

429

IF YOU were against the New Deal and its wholesale buying of pauper votes, then you were against Christian charity. If you were against the gross injustices and dishonesties of the Wagner Labor Act, then you were against labor. If you were against packing the Supreme Court, then you were in favor of letting Wall Street do it. If you are against using Dr. Quack's cancer salve, then you are in favor of letting Uncle Julius die. If you are against Holy Church, or Christian Science, then you are against God. It is an old, old argument.

430

IT IS argued that metaphysics is necessary to man, and that common sense cannot meet his needs. This is nonsense. Every man, of course, subscribes to some theory of knowledge, but usually it is very simple: he believes he knows whatever the evidence of his sense tells him. All the

acts of daily life are regulated on this basis of common
sense. We are born, live and die by it. Metaphysics in the
more pretentious sense never really enters into our lives. All
governments are run by common sense; wars are made by it;
it is at the heart of all trade, as of all science. Only religion
and poetry depart from it, and neither is a living reality to
most men. To the rest, even although they may be pious, religion is only a form. They accept it without grasping its
metaphysical structure, or even suspecting that it has such
a structure. They assume almost always that it is grounded,
like other ideas, on common sense—as it is, indeed, to a
very large extent, for every theological system tries to justify
itself on common-sense grounds. That justification may not
be its major one, but nevertheless it is an important one.

431

THE RELIGIOUS man, starting out with an outfit of irrational
postulates and untenable hopes, tries to fit them into the
facts of a harshly material world. In the process he must do
violence to both. They can never march together; indeed,
they are intrinsically irreconcilable. A common way out of
the dilemma is the resort to mysticism, which is simply
an attempt to construct a non-Euclidian world in which
anything that can be imagined is assumed to have happened.

432

MY EARLY writing was pretty bad, and it always makes me
uncomfortable, on looking into an old clipping-book, to
remember that this or that piece was regarded as well done
at the time it was written. My elders on the Baltimore

Morning Herald were quite incapable of helping me here. A few of them, notably Max Ways, the city editor, knew news when they saw it, but not one of them was a competent writer. My model in those days was the old New York *Sun,* and especially its editorial page. This model was both good and bad—good because it taught me that good sense was at the bottom of all good writing, but bad because it showed a considerable artificiality of style, and made me overestimate the value of smart phrases. For a time it caused me to forget my first idol, Thomas Henry Huxley, who was as smart as the best of them, but always put clarity first. I am still convinced that his prose was the best produced by an Englishman in the Nineteenth Century. It was as far ahead of that of Macaulay as that of Macaulay was ahead of the ornate quasi-Latin of the later Eighteenth Century. No matter how difficult the theme he dealt with, Huxley was always crystal clear. He even made metaphysics intelligible, and, what is more, charming. Nietzsche did the same thing in German, but I can recall no one else in English.

Huxley greatly influenced my early short stories, though he never wrote any fiction himself. I well recall how pleased I was when Ellery Sedgwick, then editor of *Frank Leslie's Popular Monthly,* praised the directness, simplicity and vividness of a story of mine, "The Flight of the Victor," printed in his magazine in September, 1901. I was only twenty when I wrote it. Soon afterward I succumbed to more sophisticated and tortured devices, and there was a good deal of empty ornament in my first prose book, "George Bernard Shaw: His Plays." There was also plenty of bad writing in my early *Smart Set* book reviews, begun in November, 1908. Soon afterward I began to tone down, and by the time I was thirty I had developed a style that was clear and alive. I can detect no diminution of its aliveness as I grow older. It seems to me that I can write quite as well today (1945) as I could write in 1910, though I find writing less easy than it used to be. The imbeciles who have printed acres of comment on my books have seldom noticed the chief character of my style. It is that I write with almost scientific precision—that my meaning is never obscure. The ignorant have often complained that my vocabulary is beyond them, but that is simply because my ideas cover a wider range than theirs do. Once they have consulted the dictionary they always know exactly what I intend to say. I am as far as any writer can get from the muffled sonorities of, say, John Dewey.

PRINTER'S NOTE

This book is set in ELECTRA, *a Linotype face designed by* W. A. DWIGGINS. *This face cannot be classified as either "modern" or "old-style." It is not based on any historical model, nor does it echo any particular period or style. It avoids the extreme contrast between "thick" and "thin" elements that marks most "modern" faces, and attempts to give a feeling of fluidity, power, and speed.*

The book was composed, printed, and bound by THE PLIMPTON PRESS, *Norwood, Massachusetts. The paper was made by* S. D. WARREN COMPANY, *Boston. The typography and binding are based on original designs by W. A.* DWIGGINS.